"...one of Cincinnati's most famous..."
—Joyce Rosencrans, *Cincinnati Post*

"IN THE BEGINNING...living end
...a giant tour de force of the culinary kingdom of hors d'oeuvre."
—Ann Valentine, *Houston Post*

"Some mighty good ones
...200 pages...350 recipes...many...are very simple..."
—Bernie O'Brien, *Hollywood (FL) Sun Tattler*

"...ultimate in hors d'oeuvre books"
—Jill Wolowic, *Columbus (OH) Dispatch*

"...party planning...treasure..."
—Martha Giddens, *Savannah Morning News*

"...hors d'oeuvre encyclopedia"
—Eileen Shepard, *(Albany, N.Y.) Knickerbocker News*

"Perfect for holiday party season..."
—Nancy Weir, *Florida Times-Union*

"Become...queen of appetizer makers..."
—Patricia Coffee, *Bridgeport (CT) Post*

"...braille version...innovative recipes..."
—Rosemary Vavrin, *Anchorage (AK) Times*

"One of the best"
—Lois Taylor, *Honolulu Star*

We wish to express our appreciation to the news media for their splendid cooperation and encouragement.

IN THE BEGINNING

a collection of hors d'oeuvres

Enlarged and revised
September, 1987

rockdale ridge press
8501 ridge road
cincinnati, ohio, 45236
513-891-9900

1st Printing — November, 1975
2nd Printing — January, 1976
3rd Printing — August, 1976
4th Printing — November, 1976
5th Printing — October, 1977
6th Printing — July, 1978
7th Printing — November, 1978
8th Printing — September, 1979
9th Printing — October, 1980
10th Printing — May, 1981
11th Printing — August, 1981
12th Printing — April, 1982
13th Printing — October, 1982
14th Printing — September, 1983
15th Printing — May, 1984
16th Printing — September, 1987

IN THE BEGINNING

Library of Congress Cataloging in Publication Data

Main entry under title:

IN THE BEGINNING.

Includes index.
1. Cookery (Appetizers)

TX740.15 1982	641.8'12	82-5241
ISBN 0-9602338-3-0		AACR2

Printed by
The Feicke Printing Co.
Cincinnati, Ohio

Typeset by
Reporter Typographics
Cincinnati, Ohio

FOREWORD

To all hosts and hostesses everywhere who have dreamed of a cookbook comprised of hors d'oeuvres which are elegant to serve, but easy to prepare, IN THE BEGINNING is dedicated. Here are the finest hors d'oeuvres imaginable; they have brought raves from party givers and party goers.

In order to update and enhance IN THE BEGINNING the editors have prepared a new printing with additions and revisions to add to the pleasure of using the book. A new chapter on party drinks has been included as a natural partner to hors d'oeuvres. The format of the index has been revised to provide an easier means for finding the perfect hors d'oeuvre. For quick access, recipes are listed by name, by category and by ingredients.

We are grateful that so many shared prized recipes with us and with you. Some are original creations; others have been handed down from generation to generation. All are presented in a clear, concise, step-by-step manner. The end results are superb. Only the preparations are simple.

From the time we first fancied the idea of a cookbook, we thought how exciting it would be to bring together in one handy volume all kinds of appetizers, canapés, soups, drinks and other hot and cold, delicate and hearty palate pleasers.

Now that fancy has become fact, we know that you'll agree that when it comes to hors d'oeuvres, IN THE BEGINNING is the living end!

ROCKDALE RIDGE PRESS

**Cover design and illustrations
by Alice H. Balterman**

TO THE CONTRIBUTORS

IN THE BEGINNING is dedicated to the more than one hundred fine cooks whose prized and special recipes have been handed to us and to you on a silver platter.

Without them, without their generosity and their willingness to share, IN THE BEGINNING could not have had a beginning.

Their interest and their concern, their ingredients and their culinary talents served as the Genesis of this book.

We thank them through a dedication. It is our sincere hope that your pleasure in preparing and serving their treasures will multiply the dedication thousandfold.

THE EDITORS

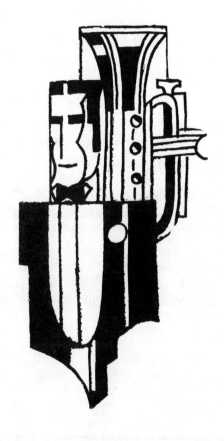

Braille Copies available on order from
National Braille Association

Braille Book Bank
1290 University Avenue
Rochester, N.Y. 14607

TABLE OF CONTENTS

FOR YOUR CONVENIENCE

You will notice throughout IN THE BEGINNING, references to recipes in BEGINNING AGAIN. For ease in use, they are noted by page number.

BEGINNING AGAIN is the sequel to IN THE BEGINNING and contains 400 more delicious hors d'oeuvre recipes.

■■■■■■■■■■■■■

Recipes suggesting use of blender may be done successfully in a food processor.

Take a Refreshing Dip

Your guests will plunge in when you serve hot and cold dips. Unique and diversified to please every palate.

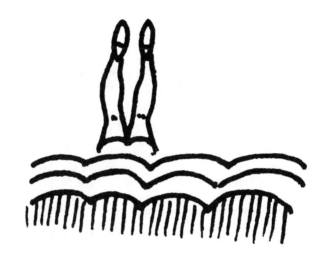

1

COLD DIPS
General Directions for Cold Dips

Mix seasonings thoroughly with mayonnaise or sour cream. Mock Sour Cream can be satisfactorily substituted for sour cream to adapt many dip recipes for low cholesterol diet. (See page 131.) Let stand several hours in refrigerator before serving to blend flavors. May be prepared ahead and stored in covered container in refrigerator for several days.

Vegetables for Dipping

Asparagus	Cucumber slices
Radishes	Cherry tomatoes
Celery	Kohlrabi
Carrot strips	Cauliflower buds
Mushrooms	Broccoli buds
Pea pods	Turnip slices

Zucchini— Peel vegetable, cut crosswise in thirds, then cut like thick french fries and salt lightly with seasoned salt just before serving.

Filled Party Loaves

Crusty round French breads, round pumpernickels or long rye breads, hollowed out make great containers for dips. The loaf can be refilled when dip is used up. The bread is particularly delicious when soaked up with the dip. The loaf itself can be cut into chunks and served when it becomes empty.

1. To prepare loaf: Cut ¾ inch slice off top of loaf. Scoop out soft bread, leaving ¾ inch shell. Cut top slice and scooped out bread into cubes to use for dipping. (Wrap to prevent drying out.)
2. Place loaf on serving platter and fill loaf with desired dip. Garnish with caviar, parsley, paprika as desired. Place cubes of bread around loaf.

Note: A day old loaf is more easily handled.

Loaf may be prepared ahead of time and stored in plastic bag in freezer or refrigerator.

Suggested Combinations:

Pumpernickel bread
Beer Dip (page 15)
Hummus Bi Tahini (page 15)
Herring Dip (page 18)
Swiss Cheese Dip (page 24)
Creamy Fish Dip (page 18)

French or Vienna Bread
Cheese and Avocado Dip (page 16)
Olivacado Dip (page 16)
Thistle Dip (page 16)
Crabmeat Dip II or III (page 19)

Beer Dip

Serves 12

1 cup beer
1 pound sharp cheddar
1¼ ounces Roquefort
2 tablespoons butter

½ medium onion
2 cloves garlic or
  1 teaspoon garlic powder
1 teaspoon Worcestershire
½ teaspoon Tabasco

1. Heat beer and cool.
2. Soften and cream together in mixer both cheeses and butter. Add the rest of the ingredients.
3. Use the beer to thin to spreading consistency.

Serve in pumpernickel Party Loaf. (See page 14.)

Hummus Bi Tahini

Chick Peas with Sesame Seed Paste

Serves 12-15 people

1 pound can chick peas
Juice of 4-6 lemons, to taste
4-6 cloves garlic, crushed
1 teaspoon salt
1 cup tahini (sesame seed paste)
1 round rye, pumpernickel or
  potato bread, unsliced

Garnish:
2 tablespoons olive oil
2 teaspoons paprika
2 tablespoons finely chopped
  parsley
10 whole chick peas

1. Drain chick peas. Put aside about 10 for garnish.
2. In electric blender, pour in lemon juice and a few drops of water. Add tahini, garlic and salt. Blend at high speed adding chick peas, a few at a time, until it reaches a consistency of a cream paste. If paste remains too thick, add water or lemon juice, a little at a time. Adjust seasoning (lemon, garlic, salt).

Note: Hollow bread. Pour hummus mixture into bread and garnish by dribbling olive oil mixed with paprika over surface of hummus. Sprinkle with chopped parsley and arrange a decorative pattern of whole chick peas on top. Cut hollowed out bread into serving cubes to be used for dipping into hummus mixture.

Note: The tahini, or sesame paste, can be purchased in any Greek food store. The paste is made from sesame meal. This recipe is most widely known and appreciated in the Middle East.

Cheese and Avocado Dip

1 8-ounce can whipped creamed
  cheese
1 ripe avocado
½ cup mayonnaise

Juice of ½ lemon
Pinch of garlic powder
Paprika

1. Beat together creamed cheese, mashed avocado, mayonnaise, lemon juice and garlic powder.
2. Put in serving bowl; sprinkle with paparika.

Suggestion: Can be made same day and put in refrigerator. Everyone raves about it.

Olivacado Dip

1 ripe avocado
1 2½-ounce can sliced or chopped
  ripe olives

½ teaspoon seasoned salt
Juice of ½ lemon or lime
1 tablespoon grated fresh onion

1. Remove flesh from avocado by scooping from skin with spoon; mash. Save shell to use for heaping back into it the finished mixture.
2. Mix flesh with well drained olives, onion, seasoned salt and lime or lemon juice.
3. Heap back into avocado shells.

Note: Serve with crisp slices of fresh carrot, turnip, radish, kohirabi or other fresh vegetables. (Worth trying unusual ones.)

Thistle Dip

Makes 1½ cups

1 6-ounce jar marinated artichoke
  hearts
1 cup sour cream

½ teaspoon onion salt
Dash cayenne pepper

1. Place artichokes with liquid in blender. Cover and blend, scraping down sides as needed until completely smooth.
2. Transfer to bowl. Stir in remaining ingredients.
3. Refrigerate at least 1 hour.

Note: Serve with crackers, potato chips, or vegetables.

Spinach Dip

1 package frozen, chopped spinach
½ cup chopped scallions
½ cup finely minced parsley
2 cups Hellman's or Best Foods
  mayonnaise
  (do not use any other brand)

1 teaspoon salt
⅛ teaspoon freshly ground pepper

1. Thaw spinach and squeeze out liquid.
2. Mix all ingredients together and chill for 24 hours.

Note: Excellent with raw vegetables. "One of the best vegetable dips."

Spinach Nancy

1 package frozen, chopped spinach
2 tablespoons mayonnaise

Pinch garlic salt
⅛ teaspoon red pepper
½ teaspoon lemon juice

1. Cook and drain spinach as directed on package.
2. Mix with remaining ingredients and season to taste.

It's easy! Folks like it. Make a day ahead. Serve in small bowl surrounded with small crackers or party rye.

Pesto Leonardo

⅔ cup fresh basil leaves
⅓ cup fresh flat Italian parsley
½ cup olive oil
4 cloves garlic, minced
⅓ cup pignoli (pine nuts)

½ cup Parmesan, fresh grated
1 teaspoon fresh grated black
  pepper
1 cup ricotta cheese

1. Chop parsley and basil a little. Put in blender with 2 tablespoons olive oil and garlic. Blend until you have a green paste.
2. Add pine nuts and 2 tablespoons more of the olive oil. Blend 2 minutes. Add remaining ingredients and blend until smooth and well mixed.

Not for the fainthearted!

A spicy dip for vegetables or crackers.

Make in summer using fresh basil.

Freezes well.

Serve as a sauce for pasta. Warm but do not boil. Serve over fettucini or cavatelli. Top with grated Romano. **17**

Herring Dip

12-ounce jar herring
2 tablespoons dehydrated onion
2 teaspoons sugar

1 pint sour cream
2 teaspoons mustard seed
½ cup chopped tart apple

1. Drain herring on paper towels.
2. Chop herring and mix with remaining ingredients.

Make a day ahead.

Creamy Fish Dip

*1 pound jar gefilte fish in liquid
  broth
3 tablespoons fish broth
1 teaspoon lemon juice

2 teaspoons prepared white
  horseradish
½ teaspoon salt
Dash pepper

1. Drain fish, reserving broth.
2. Blend fish with remaining ingredients in blender.
3. Refrigerate for about one hour.

Note: Serve with crackers.

**A quick and easy method to make your own gelfite fish can be
found on page 115 of BEGINNING AGAIN.*

Green Goddess Dip

Serves 6

1 clove garlic, minced
1 2-ounce can anchovies, chopped
3 tablespoons chopped chives or
1 tablespoon dehydrated chives
1 tablespoon vinegar

½ cup sour cream
1 cup mayonnaise
⅓ cup chopped parsley
  or
3 tablespoons dehydrated parsley

Put all ingredients in the blender and blend until smooth. (A
little milk may be added if it seems to be too thick.)

*This dip is fantastic when served with fresh cut-up vegetables. If
there is any left over, use it as a salad dressing. It may be made
a day or two ahead and refrigerated.*

Crabmeat Dip I

Serves 6

1 cup smooth cottage cheese
1 teaspoon Worcestershire
2 teaspoons dill weed
*1 can crabmeat
2 tablespoons buttermilk

1 tablespoon lemon juice
½ teaspoon salt
Freshly ground pepper
2 teaspoons mustard seed
¼ cup chopped, drained cucumber

1. Combine all ingredients, adding more buttermilk if necessary to obtain good consistency.
2. Season to taste. Makes 2¼ cups.

Prepare 6-8 hours in advance to allow time for mustard seed to soften.

A good low calorie dip.

Crabmeat Dip II

Serves 12 or so

1 pint sour cream
1 package onion soup mix

*1 7½-ounce can crabmeat

1. Pick shell and bones from crab meat.
2. Mix together with cream and soup mix until well blended.

Should be made several hours ahead and chilled. Serve with crackers or potato chips.

Crabmeat Dip III

*2 6-ounce boxes frozen Alaska
   King Crab
½ cup Hellman's mayonnaise

½ cup sour cream
½ cup chopped celery

Thaw crab. Mix with remaining ingredients.

Serve with crackers or party rye. Make as much as you can afford. It won't be left over!

*See page 26.

Shrimp Dip I

Serves 16

1 8-ounce package cream cheese
1 cup tomato catsup
2 tablespoons grated onion

½ teaspoon prepared mustard
½ to ¾ pound shrimp, cut up
Tabasco, salt and paprika to taste

1. Soften cheese and combine all ingredients in electric blender.
2. Chill.

Serve with melba toast.

Shrimp Dip II

Serves 4

1 3-ounce package cream cheese
½ cup shrimp, cut fine
3 tablespoons cocktail sauce

Dash A-1 sauce
Salt and pepper to taste

1. Cream cheese until soft (add a little milk). Mash in shrimp.
2. Add cocktail sauce, A-1 sauce, salt and pepper. Blend until proper consistency to spread (adding milk or more cocktail sauce).

Can be made ahead. Use crackers or vegetables for dipping.

Sour Cream Shrimp Dip

Makes 1½ cups

1 5-ounce can shrimp, drained
1 cup sour cream
¼ cup chili sauce
2 teaspoons lemon juice

½ teaspoon salt
⅛ teaspoon pepper
1 teaspoon horseradish
Dash Tabasco

Cut shrimp into small pieces and mix with other ingredients.

Note: Use as spread or dip.

Shrimp Cheese Dip

Makes about 2 cups

¼ cup milk
½ cup mayonnaise
1 5-ounce can shrimp, drained
1 small onion, cut up

1 cup cubed cheddar
1 tablespoon Worcestershire
¼ teaspoon garlic salt
3 drops hot pepper sauce

1. Put all ingredients in a blender and blend until smooth.
2. Chill.

Serve with crackers to dip.

Provencal Canapé Spread (or Dip)

Serves 6

4 tablespoons mayonnaise
2 tablespoons oil (olive or
vegetable or half of each)
1 tablespoon prepared mustard
(mild)
1 medium Spanish onion, finely
chopped

10 anchovy fillets, finely chopped
2 hard boiled eggs, finely chopped
1 lemon (juice and rind)
Freshly ground black pepper

1. Combine and beat until smooth the mayonnaise, oil and
mustard.
2. Add remaining ingredients (may not need all the lemon juice;
therefore, add this as needed for taste and consistency.)

*A very delicately flavored dish which should not be overwhelmed
by savory breads. Serve on buttered round of Italian bread. This
can also be served as a dip, with Devonshire Toasts.*

Pink Devil Dip

Makes 1 cup

1 cup sour cream
2 tablespoons chili sauce
¼ teaspoon prepared horseradish

1 4-ounce can deviled ham
1 teaspoon instant minced onion

1. Combine all ingredients in a small bowl and stir to blend well.
2. Cover and chill one hour.

Serve as a dip with potato chips or corn chips.

Surprise Dip

Serves 10-12

1 can tomato soup, undiluted
Dash of Tabasco
Dash of onion powder

½ cup mayonnaise
Dash of Worcestershire
Dash of garlic powder

Mix all ingredients together well.

Serve with potato chips or as a salad dressing.

Tastes like a cheese dip; most guests can't guess the ingredients.

Quick Dips

Caviar Dip

1 cup sour cream — Small jar caviar

Curry Dip I

1 cup mayonnaise — Curry powder, to taste (1 to 3 teaspoons)

Curry Dip II

1 cup mayonnaise
1 tablespoon tarragon powder
1 teaspoon horseradish

1 teaspoon dehydrated onion
1 teaspoon garlic salt
1 teaspoon curry powder

Nippy Dip

1 cup sour cream
3 cups Hellman's or Best Food's mayonnaise
2 tablespoons chopped capers, drained
½ cup frozen chopped chives

1 clove garlic, crushed
½ cup chopped parsley (or 2-3 tablespoons dehydrated)
1 teaspoon Tabasco
1 to 3 teaspoons horseradish, to taste

A Quick Dip

1 cup mayonnaise — 1½ teaspoons tarragon vinegar

Onion Soup Dip

1 package onion soup mix — 2 cups sour cream

1. Blend onion soup mix with sour cream.
2. Chill.

Note: This is one of the oldest of dips. It is tasty and easy for emergencies. Serve surrounded by potato chips or vegetables for dipping.

Vegetable Dip

1 cup sour cream
1 cup mayonnaise
2 tablespoons Beau Monde seasoning

1 tablespoon dill weed
1 teaspoon grated onion (optional)
1 teaspoon parsley

Combine all ingredients, blending thoroughly.

Serve as a dip with assorted vegetables.

Tangy Clam Dip

1 can New England Clam Chowder
(undiluted)
2 heaping tablespoons minced
onions

2 tablespoons catsup
1 8-ounce package cream cheese
½ teaspoon horseradish

Put into blender until smooth.

Refrigerate until ready to use. Serve with chips, celery, or cauliflower.

Tomato Clam Dip

Makes 2 cups

1 pint sour cream
1 7½-ounce can minced clams,
drained

1 1½-ounce envelope spaghetti
sauce mix

1. Combine all ingredients in a small bowl and blend well.
2. Cover and chill one hour.

Serve as a dip with potato chips or crackers.

Low Calorie Clam Dip

Serves 6

1½ cups smooth cottage cheese
1 tablespoon lemon juice
¼ teaspoon grated onion
1-2 teaspoons clam juice

1-2 tablespoons buttermilk
Salt and pepper to taste
1 7½-ounce can well drained
minced clams

1. Combine all ingredients, adding enough liquid to obtain good
consistency.
2. Correct seasonings.

Serve with vegetables for dipping.

Clam Dip

Makes 1¼ cups

1 7-ounce can minced clams
½ teaspoon finely diced onion
½ teaspoon salt

⅛ teaspoon pepper
2 3-ounce packages cream cheese,
broken in pieces

1. Drain clams, reserving broth.
2. Put onions, clams, 2 tablespoons clam broth, seasonings and
cream cheese in blender. Cover; blend until just mixed
3. Chill before serving.

Note: Can be made ahead. Serve with carrot sticks, celery or potato chips.

Yogurt Vegetable Dip
Low Calorie

Makes 1 cup

½ cup smooth cottage cheese
1 tablespoon finely grated carrot
2 teaspoons finely grated onion
1 teaspoon finely grated green
   pepper

½ teaspoon salt
⅛ teaspoon garlic salt
Dash white pepper
1 cup plain yogurt

1. Beat cottage cheese in a small bowl, using a fork.
2. Add remaining ingredients, except yogurt, and mix well.
3. Fold in yogurt, cover and chill.

Serve with raw vegetables and chips.

Herb Yogurt Dip
Low Calorie

Makes 1 cup

1 teaspoon caraway seed
1 tablespoon chopped green onion

1 cup plain yogurt
¼ teaspoon basil leaves, crushed

1. Pour boiling water over caraway seed and let stand 5 minutes, then drain.
2. To yogurt, add caraway seed, green onion and basil.
3. Chill several hours.

Serve with raw vegetables.

Swiss Cheese Dip

½ cup mayonnaise
2 tablespoons chili sauce
1 cup creamed cottage cheese
1 small wedge onion, chopped

¼ teaspoon salt
¼ teaspoon celery salt
1 cup cubed Swiss cheese

1. Place all ingredients, except Swiss cheese, in blender. Blend on high until smooth.
2. Add cheese a little at a time until blended.

HOT DIPS

Chili con Queso

Serves about 8

1 pound American cheese
1 4-ounce can diced green chilies

1 pound can whole tomatoes
1 tablespoon minced onion

1. Cut cheese into small cubes.
2. Drain tomatoes and then chop fine; reserve liquid.
3. Add all ingredients to a chafing dish or double boiler and heat to melt cheese and mix ingredients. Adjust thickness using reserved tomato juice to give smooth dip consistency. Add more chilies if hotter taste is desired.

For fire eaters the whole can of green chilies can be used. Otherwise, start with no more than ¼-½ can of chilies (balance can be frozen).

Can be made ahead. Serve hot from chafing dish with corn chips (tortilla chips.)

Hot Brie

Serves 16-20

*1 whole Brie cheese, well ripened
(2 pounds)

1 cup slivered almonds

1. Place cheese in oven-proof serving dish. Sprinkle almonds over top.
2. Bake in 300° oven for 20 minutes (until cheese is soft and almonds brown).

Serve with assorted crackers. A delectable delight.

Easy elegance.

A whole small canned Brie may be substituted. Use ⅓ cup almonds and reduce baking time to 15 minutes.

Hot Crabmeat Dip

½ pound processed American
cheese
½ cup butter or margarine

*1 7½-ounce can crabmeat
Sherry

1. Melt cheese and butter in top of double boiler. Stir hard until blended.
2. Mix in drained crabmeat and enough sherry to give spreading consistency.

Note: Serve in chafing dish with crackers.

Hot Crab Spread

*2 6-ounce packages frozen or
2 7½-ounce cans crabmeat,
    drained
2 8-ounce packages cream cheese
½ cup mayonnaise
1 bunch green onions, chopped

2 dashes hot red pepper sauce
1 teaspoon Worcestershire
Handful of slivered almonds

1. Mix all together, reserving almonds for topping.
2. Place in bake and serve dish and bake at 350° for 20 minutes.

Note: Serve with crackers.

Hot Crabmeat Soufflé Dip

*1 7½-ounce can crabmeat,
    drained
1 8-ounce package cream cheese
1 teaspoon horseradish

1 8-ounce container sour cream
Pinch of sugar
Lemon juice to taste

1. Flake crabmeat and add to softened cream cheese. Mix with other ingredients.
2. Bake ½ hour at 350° in 1 quart soufflé dish.

---

*   *SUGGESTIONS FOR PREPARING CRABMEAT*
For crab dishes using canned or frozen crab, pick it over carefully for pieces of bone and shell.

Casa Pecan Spread

1 8-ounce package cream cheese, softened
2 teaspoons milk
2½ ounces dried beef, chopped
¼ cup finely chopped green peppers
2 tablespoons dehydrated onion flakes

½ teaspoon garlic salt
½ teaspoon pepper
½ cup dairy sour cream
½ cup coarsely chopped pecans
1 tablespoon butter or margarine
½ teaspoon salt

1. Combine softened cream cheese and milk, mixing until well blended.
2. Stir in dried beef, onion flakes, green peppers and seasoning; mix well. Fold in sour cream.
3. Spoon into 8 inch pie plate or small baking dish.
4. Heat and crisp pecans in melted butter or margarine and salt. Sprinkle over cheese mixture.
5. Bake at 350° for 20 minutes.

Serve hot with crackers. Can be assembled the night before and refrigerated. Bake when ready to serve.

Note: Casserole should be at room temperature before placing in oven to prevent cracking.

Hot Shrimp Dip

1 can cream of shrimp soup
1 5-ounce can shrimp
1 4-ounce can mushrooms cut into pieces (drained)

1 tablespoon Parmesan cheese
1 teaspoon Worcestershire
1 tablespoon chopped parsley

1. Mix all ingredients together.
2. Heat in saucepan.

Note: Serve in small fondue pot with melba rounds.

FONDUES

General Directions

1. Two types of cheese used in fondues are Emmentaler and Gruyére. Emmentaler is milder and is used for a mild tasting fondue. Half Emmentaler and half Gruyére can be used for a stronger tasting fondue and Gruyére cheese alone makes the strongest flavor. Use a well-aged cheese to prevent stringy fondue.
2. The cheese melts more smoothly when cut into very small pieces or shredded, not grated.
3. The type of wine used is important. It should be light, lively, dry white wine such as Chablis, Riesling, Neuchatel or Rhine. If the wine is not tart enough, add a little lemon juice, about 1½ teaspoons for every half pound of cheese. Kirsch (cherry brandy) is the most popular liqueur used in making fondue, but brandy, cognac, light white rum or apple jack may be used or the liqueur omitted.
4. Keep mixture bubbling lightly. If the fondue gets too thick while being served add a little wine that has been warmed first. If it separates or gets lumpy, put the fondue back on the stove and stir in ½ teaspoon cornstarch blended with a little warm wine, then stir with a whisk until smooth.
5. Spear bread chunks on fondue fork and dunk with stirring motion.
6. A pottery fondue pot is the best type of container as it produces an even heat and prevents curdled and stringy fondue.

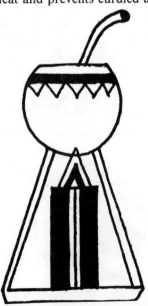

Cheese Fondue

Serves 6 to 8

1½ pounds Emmentaler, shredded
4 tablespoons flour
3 cups dry white wine
2 cloves of garlic, peeled and cut
   in half
½ teaspoon salt

Pinch white pepper
Dash nutmeg
2 tablespoons kirsch, brandy or
   cognac
Bite-sized pieces of French bread

1. Dredge cheese with flour.
2. In a metal or glass ovenproof sauce pan, put in wine and set over low heat. Heat until bubbles rise to surface and stir with a wooden spoon or fork or silver fork. (Important: do not let wine reach boiling point.)
3. Add cheese, a little at a time, while continuing to stir. Keep stirring until mixture is bubbling lightly.
4. Rub bottom and sides of an earthenware 2-quart casserole of fondue pot with garlic cloves. Set on heating element.
5. Add seasonings and kirsch to cheese mixture; blend well and pour into casserole.

For onion-cheese fondue: Add 1 envelope (1⅔ ounces) dry onion soup mix to wine before heating. Omit salt, pepper and nutmeg.

Cheddar Cheese Fondue

Makes 2 cups

¼ cup butter or margarine
¼ cup flour
1 teaspoon MSG
½ teaspoon salt
¼ teaspoon dry mustard

1 12-ounce can beer
1½ teaspoons Worcestershire
2 cups (½ pound) shredded sharp
   cheddar cheese
Bite-size pieces pumpernickel bread

1. Melt shortening in saucepan and blend in flour, MSG, salt and dry mustard.
2. Slowly add beer and Worcestershire.
3. Cook, stirring constantly, until mixture thickens and comes to a boil.
4. Add cheese; cook, stirring constantly, until melted.
5. Keep warm in a fondue dish.

Serve with chunks of pumpernickel bread speared on forks.

Bacon and Cheese Fondue

Makes 1½ cups

4 slices bacon, cooked, drained
    and crumbled
1 8-ounce can tomato sauce with
    onions
⅛ teaspoon garlic salt

⅛ teaspoon pepper
½ cup shredded cheddar
Bite size pieces of French bread

1. Combine bacon and tomato sauce, garlic salt and pepper and simmer for 5 minutes.
2. Add cheese, stirring constantly until melted and smooth.

Serve in fondue dish, with chunks of French bread for dunking.

Swiss Cheese Fondue

Serves 8

1 clove garlic
1 cup Chablis, or any dry white
    wine
1 pound Swiss cheese, grated

1 tablespoon cornstarch mixed
    with little water
2 tablespoons kirsch

1. Rub earthenware fondue pot or ovenproof dish with garlic.
2. Place pot over burner, pour in wine and warm it.
3. Add grated cheese. Stir constantly with wooden spoon until cheese melts.
4. Add cornstarch water to cheese, stirring constantly until thickened.
5. Before serving add Kirsch.

Note: Serve in chafing dish or fondue dish with French bread cubed, toasted and speared on a fork to dip in fondue.

Spreading Joy

Cheese ball, pâté and a myriad of tantalizing spreads to tempt the taste buds.

2

CHEESE BALLS AND LOGS

Use your imagination in shaping these cheese mixtures. But remember, once guests start digging in, the log stays neater than the ball.

Cheese Log

1 pound sharp cheddar, shredded
1 cup chopped pecans
1 clove garlic, mashed

1 8-ounce package cream cheese
Chili powder

1. Have cheeses at room temperature. Blend with pecans and garlic.
2. Make into 2 rolls, about the diameter of a silver dollar. Roll in chili powder on a piece of waxed paper until heavily coated.
3. Chill.

Serve with assorted crackers.
May be made ahead and either refrigerated or frozen.

Cheese Ball Hors d'Oeuvre

Makes 1-2 lb. cheese balls

2 8-ounce packages sharp cheddar
2 8-ounce packages American cheese
2 3-ounce packages cream cheese
2 tablespoons Worcestershire

1 teaspoon hot pepper sauce
2 large cloves garlic, pressed
1 tablespoon chili powder
1 tablespoon paprika

1. Grate cheddar and American cheese in mixing bowl. Blend cheeses together until there are no lumps.
2. Add cream cheese.
3. Add Worcestershire, hot pepper sauce and garlic. Blend.
4. Place in refrigerator until firm enough to form one large or two smaller balls. Roll the ball in the chili powder and paprika that have been mixed together.

Store in refrigerator, wrapped in waxed paper, until ready to serve. It will keep fresh for a week. Place on large platter. Tuck parsley or watercress around base of ball. Surround by assortment of crackers.

Salmon Party Log

1 1-pound can salmon
¼ teaspoon salt
3 tablespoons snipped parsley
2 teaspoons grated onion
1 cup chopped pecans

1 8-ounce package cream cheese, softened
¼ teaspoon liquid smoke
1 tablespoon lemon juice
1 teaspoon horseradish

1. Drain salmon well. Bone and flake.
2. Combine everything except parsley and nuts. Chill several hours.
3. Roll in log (heavy wax paper helps).
4. Roll log in nuts and parsley, or just in parsley.

Serve with party rye bread.
Keeps in refrigerator for days.

Cheese Olive Roll

½ pound bleu cheese
1 8-ounce package cream cheese
¼ cup butter
1 tablespoon minced chives

1 tablespoon brandy
½ cup minced ripe olives
Chopped toasted almonds

1. Cream together bleu cheese and cream cheese with butter.
2. Add chives, brandy and minced ripe olives.
3. Form mixture into a roll, cover with almonds and chill.
4. Slice and serve with toasted crackers.

Roquefort Cheese Ball

4 ounces Roquefort
6 ounces sharp cheddar
1 3-ounce package cream cheese
1 teaspoon MSG

1-2 teaspoons onion salt
½ teaspoon Worcestershire
¾ cup finely chopped nutmeats (preferably walnuts)

1. Allow cheeses to stay at room temperature to soften.
2. Mix with seasonings and ½ cup nutmeats; blend well.
3. Place mixture on wax paper and shape into a ball.
4. Refrigerate for 1-2 hours and then roll ball in the remaining ¼ cup nutmeats.

Refrigerate until one hour before serving time. Use as a spread on crackers or icebox rye.

Mystery Cheese Ball

Makes 3 cheese balls

2 pounds Old English cheese, shredded
1 5-ounce jar bleu cheese spread

1 8-ounce package cream cheese
Chopped nuts or parsley

1. Leave cheeses at room temperature and then blend in electric mixer.
2. Shape into 3 large balls. Roll in chopped nuts or parsley.

Will feed an army!

May be frozen.

Serve at room temperature.

Zingy Ham Butter Ball

Makes 5 inch ball

3 tablespoons dehydrated bell pepper
⅓ cup tarragon vinegar
3 tablespoons Mei Yen seasoning
2 tablespoons dry mustard

2 sticks butter
2½ tablespoons onion powder
1 cup (8 ounces) ground ham

1. Soak bell peppers in vinegar for 15 minutes.
2. Cream together butter and seasonings.
3. Mix ham with all above ingredients.
4. Form into ball.

Make ahead. Keeps several days.

Cream Cheese Beef Log

Serves 6 to 8

1 8-ounce package cream cheese
⅓ cup Parmesan cheese

⅓ cup chopped olives
3 ounces chipped beef

1. Combine all ingredients except beef, mixing well.
2. Chop beef into small pieces.
3. Roll cheese into log shape.
4. Roll cheese log in beef pieces, covering well.

The chipped beef is a nice change. Make a day ahead — serve with assorted crackers.

Tomato Cheese Log

Serves 10

⅓ cup tomato paste
1 8-ounce package cream cheese, softened
8 ounces cheddar, grated
½ cup butter or margarine

2 tablespoons dehydrated chopped onion
2 cloves garlic, crushed
1 teaspoon salt
⅛ to ¼ teaspoon cayenne pepper
8 ounces chopped walnuts

1. Combine all ingredients except walnuts; beat with electric mixer.
2. Spoon out onto a large piece of wax paper. Roll with wax paper to form log.
3. Place in freezer one hour or until firm.
4. Cover with chopped walnuts.
5. Place on platter and serve as an appetizer. Serve very cold.

Stuffed Edam Cheese

1 Edam cheese (7-8 ounces)
¼ cup butter
½ teaspoon dry mustard
Dash Tabasco

¼ cup chopped green olives
2 teaspoons dehydrated minced onion
2 teaspoons dry wine
2 teaspoons caraway seed

1. Cut top from Edam cheese. Scoop out inside and blend with remaining ingredients.
2. Pack back into shell.

Serve with crackers or ice box rye. The red wax shell makes a colorful container. No dish to wash.

For easier handling: Remove celophane while cheese is cold. Leave at room temperature for several hours before trying to scoop cheese out of wax shell.

Bleu Cheese Ball

1 3-ounce package cream cheese
1 3-ounce package cream cheese with chives
2 ounces bleu cheese

⅛ cup butter
⅓ cup drained chopped black olives
½ cup chopped nuts

1. Soften cheeses and butter, mix with olives, and chill.
2. Shape into ball and roll in chopped nuts.

SPREADS

Crab Meat or Shrimp Spread

Serves 12

2 8-ounce packages cream cheese
1 small onion diced very fine
½ cup mayonnaise
1 tablespoon lemon juice
1 teaspoon garlic salt

1 tablespoon Worcestershire
½ bottle chili sauce
*1 6-ounce box frozen crabmeat or
   1 package small frozen cooked
   shrimp

1. Soften cream cheese at room temperature.
2. Add all remaining ingredients except seafood and chili sauce. Blend.
3. Shape into oval or square on flat serving plate and cover with plastic wrap. Refrigerate overnight.
4. Right before serving, cover with chili sauce, then place shredded drained crabmeat or whole shrimps on top of chili sauce so that entire mold is covered.

*See page 26.

Shrimp Mold

2 5-ounce cans shrimp, drained
1 8-ounce package cream cheese
1 garlic bud, grated or pressed
   through garlic press

½ teaspoon Worcestershire
1 teaspoon lemon juice
1 tablespoon mayonnaise

1. Grease mold with oil and drain.
2. Mix all ingredients together. Pack into greased mold.
3. Chill overnight in mold.
4. Unmold on a serving plate.

This recipe can be doubled and placed in a fish mold.

Shrimp Spread

1 8-ounce package frozen baby
   shrimp (cooked)
1 8-ounce package cream cheese
½ cup margarine
1 can cream of shrimp soup

4 chopped green onions
Lemon juice
Worcestershire
Garlic powder
Curry powder

1. Thaw and drain frozen shrimp (be certain all excess moisture is absorbed on paper toweling).
2. In mixing bowl beat cream cheese, margarine, and cream of shrimp soup.
3. Add seasoning to taste and green onions.
4. Fold in shrimp. Press into mold or form.

Make a day ahead. Serve with assorted crackers or melba toast.

Chipped Beef Spread

Serves 4 to 6

3 ounces chipped beef
1 3-ounce package cream cheese
1 teaspoon chopped parsley
1 small sweet pickle, chopped

1 tablespoon mayonnaise
Few drops onion juice
Dash garlic salt or powder
1 tablespoon Worcestershire

Chop or dice beef and blend well with softened cream cheese, mayonnaise and seasonings.

Serve with party rye and assorted crackers.

May be thinned with sour cream to make an excellent dip.

Salmon Avocado Spread

Makes 2 cups

1 7¾-ounce can red salmon
1 ripe avocado
1 tablespoon olive or salad oil

1 clove garlic, finely chopped
1½ teaspoons grated onion
½ teaspoon salt
4 drops of Tabasco

1. Drain salmon; remove skin and flake.
2. Peel avocado, remove seed and mash.
3. Combine all ingredients and toss lightly.

Serve spread on crackers.

Salmon Mold

Serves 8-10

½ pound canned salmon
1 8-ounce package cream cheese, softened
½ teaspoon horseradish
2 teaspoons grated onion

¼ teaspoon salt
½ teaspoon liquid smoke
1 tablespoon lemon juice
¼ cup chopped parsley
1 cup chopped pecans

1. Drain salmon, remove skin and flake.
2. Mix all ingredients except parsley and pecans; shape in ball.
3. Roll in chopped parsley and chopped pecans.

Serve with crackers or party rye.

Tuna Pâté

Makes 3 cups

1 8-ounce package cream cheese
2 tablespoons chili sauce
2 tablespoons snipped parsley

1 teaspoon instant minced onion
½ teaspoon Tabasco
2 7-ounce cans tuna, drained

1. Blend softened cream cheese, chili sauce, parsley, onion and hot pepper sauce; gradually stir in drained tuna. Beat until mixture is thoroughly blended.
2. Pack in a 4 cup mold or small bowl.
3. Chill thoroughly, at least 3 hours or overnight.

At serving time, unmold on serving plate. If desired, garnish with sliced green olives. Serve with assorted crackers.

Mustard Sardine Spread

Serves 8

3 hard boiled eggs
1 tablespoon grated onion
1 tablespoon mayonnaise

1 can mustard sardines, drained
1 teaspoon vinegar
Prepared mustard and pepper to taste

1. Mash sardines and egg.
2. Add remaining ingredients.
3. Refrigerate a few hours.

Serve with party rye bread or crackers.
Does not taste like sardines. It is always fun to have your guests guess.

Anchovy Spread

1 8-ounce package cream cheese
2 tablespoons milk

1 can flat anchovies
1 very small onion, grated

1. Blend softened cream cheese with milk.
2. Add drained chopped anchovies and grated onion; mix well.

Serve with melba toast.

Pickled Shad Roe Spread

1 can shad roe
Juice of one lemon
2 tablespoons olive oil
Celery salt

Ground black pepper
Onion salt
Garlic salt

1. Devein and remove all skin from shad roe (save juice). Crumble roe with fingers so that all eggs are separated.
2. Add juice from can and remaining ingredients, adding seasoning to taste.
3. Chill for several hours.

Some say this is better than caviar.

Mock Boursin au Poivre

1 8-ounce package cream cheese
1 clove garlic, crushed
1 teaspoon caraway seed
1 teaspoon basil

1 teaspoon dill weed
1 teaspoon chopped chives,
   dehydrated
Lemon pepper

1. Blend softened cream cheese with garlic, caraway, basil, dill weed and chives.
2. Pat into round flat shape.
3. Roll generously on all sides in lemon pepper.

Note: Make a few days ahead. Serve with assorted crackers. Tastes like French Boursin au Poivre. This spread gets instant raves.

Crabmeat Pie

6-8 servings

1 8-ounce package cream cheese
*1 7½-ounce can crabmeat
1 bottle chili sauce

Dash Tabasco
Parsley — either fresh chopped or
dried

1. Soften cream cheese and mash down to ⅛ to ¼″ thick in shape of a circle on serving plate.
2. Pick over well-drained crabmeat and make sure all hard pieces of shell, etc. are removed. Break up into flakes and sprinkle in a thick layer over cream cheese.
3. Drain chili sauce of extra liquid and add Tabasco and mix. Pour mixture on cream cheese and crabmeat layers.
4. Cover with parsley so that the red layer is covered by a green layer.
5. Take 4 paper napkins, roll each up in roll to catch liquid which will drain. Allow hors d'oeuvre to drain with napkins in place until ready to serve.
6. Remove napkins and serve with crackers.

Mock Cheesecake

Don't let the title fool you—it isn't cake and there's no real cheese—but the flavor is delicious! Can be made a day ahead.

Serves 6 to 8

1 cup sour cream
¼ cup finely chopped green
  pepper
¼ cup finely chopped celery
2 tablespoons chopped pimiento
  stuffed olives
2 tablespoons chopped onion

1 teaspoon lemon juice
½ teaspoon Worcestershire
Dash paprika
2 to 3 drops hot pepper sauce
⅔ cup cheese cracker crumbs (approximately 16 crackers)

1. Combine all ingredients except cracker crumbs.
2. Line 2½ cup bowl with plastic wrap.
3. Spread ½ cup sour cream mixture in bowl.
4. Reserve ¼ cup cracker crumbs for garnish.
5. Add layer of ½ of remaining crumbs.
6. Repeat layers of sour cream mixture and cracker crumbs.
7. Chill overnight.
8. Turn out on serving plate, remove plastic wrap and top with reserved crumbs.

Note: For a more pungent flavor, mix 2-4 ounces of Roquefort, bleu or Gorgonzola with sour cream at step 3. Serve with assorted crackers and vegetables.

*See page 26.

Gorgonzola Cheese Spread

¾ pound butter
¾ pound Gorgonzola

1 teaspoon onion salt
⅛ teaspoon paprika

1. Soften butter and cheese. Blend all ingredients.
2. Put in serving dish or shape into log.

An interesting spread made of a seldom used cheese.

Camembert Spread

1. Chill equal amounts of Camembert and butter; cut them into small pieces and combine them.
2. Add finely chopped onion to taste and a generous sprinkling of paprika.
3. Mix the ingredients until they hold together. (The texture should be chunky.)
4. Shape the mixture into a mound on a serving dish.

Sherry Cheese Pâté

Serves 12

2 3-ounce packages cream cheese
4 ounces sharp cheddar, grated
2 tablespoons dry sherry
½ teaspoon curry powder

¼ teaspoon salt
1 8-ounce jar chutney
2 green onions and tops

1. Chop chutney coarsely in blender; reserve.
2. Mix cheese, wine and seasonings thoroughly.
3. Put on pie plate and chill.
4. Spread chutney over top of cheese and sprinkle with finely chopped green onions.

An interesting combination of flavors.

Liptauer Cheese

1 3-ounce glass Old English cheese
1 3-ounce package cream cheese

3 tablespoons chili sauce
1 teaspoon paprika

Blend all ingredients until well mixed.

Bleu Cheese Caviar Spread

Serves 12

2 8-ounce packages cream cheese
4 ounces bleu cheese or Roquefort
Onion powder, to taste
3 or 4 tablespoons milk to soften

2 tablespoons lemon juice
1 tablespoon caraway seed
Small jar caviar

1. Blend all ingredients except caviar.
2. Form into mound; make indentation in center and fill with caviar.

Watercress Spread

1 bunch watercress
1 8-ounce package cream cheese
1 3-ounce package cream cheese

1½ teaspoons horseradish
Dash of Worcestershire

1. Finely chop watercress leaves.
2. Soften cream cheese. Mix all ingredients together.
3. Form into round ball.

Garnish with sprigs of parsley. Serve with miniature caraway rye.

Low Calorie Cheese Spread

Serves 6 or more

1 8-ounce package Neufchatel
   cheese (low calorie)
2-3 tablespoons Worcestershire

1. Place cheese in serving dish. Allow cheese to soften 4-5 hours.
2. Pour Worcestershire over cheese.

A very easy, tasty low calorie spread, it is originally from New Orleans.

Note: Serve surrounded by carrot strips for dipping or as a spread with crackers.

Cheese in a Crock

2 cups assorted leftover cheeses
2 tablespoons cream cheese
2 tablespoons butter
2 tablespoons Scotch whiskey

4 tablespoons olive butter or
  chopped green olives
1 tablespoon caraway seed
Dash of cayenne
2 tablespoons olive oil

1. Grate enough cheese to make 2 cups. Combine with remaining ingredients and stir until smooth.
2. Pack into crock. Leave in refrigerator for 2 days or more before serving. This spread keeps for weeks and improves with aging.
3. Allow cheese to set out of refrigerator 1 hour before serving.

Serve in crock, surrounded by green grapes and assorted crackers.

This is a great way to use up odds and ends of cheeses.
Replenish crock with more cheese and seasonings as needed.

Ingwiller Fromage

Serves 10-12
Makes 1½ cups

1 8-ounce package cream cheese
  (room temperature)
½ green pepper, minced
1 small onion, minced
1 clove garlic, minced
1 tablespoon olive oil

2 tablespoons caraway seed
2 tablespoons red paprika
¼ teaspoon dry mustard
1-2-ounce can anchovies,
  undrained
Sour or sweet cream (to thin to
  spreading consistency)

1. Mix all ingredients until thoroughly blended.
2. Store in crock in refrigerator until ready to serve.

Note: Can be made ahead and refrigerated indefinitely. This is a soft, creamy spread for crackers.

Chablis Spread

Makes ¾ cup

1 3-ounce package cream cheese
1 clove garlic, crushed

2 ounces Liederkranz cheese
1 tablespoon chablis

1. Work together all ingredients until smooth.
2. Cover tightly and refrigerate for 2 days.

Egg Salad Mold

Serves 24

18 hard boiled eggs
½ cup chopped green pepper
⅓ cup finely cut celery
2 tablespoons chopped parsley
1 medium onion, minced

¼ cup diced pimiento
2-8-ounce packages cream cheese
½ cup mayonnaise
3 tablespoons chili sauce
Salt and pepper to taste

1. Shell eggs and mash.
2. Add green pepper, pimiento, celery, parsley, and onion.
3. Mash cheese, stir in mayonnaise and chili sauce.
4. Combine with vegetables and cooled mashed eggs. Season well with salt and pepper.
5. Pack into a greased ring mold and chill it for four hours.

Loosen around the edge with a spatula and turn it out upside down on a chop plate. Fill the center with cherry tomatoes. Surround with crackers or party rye bread slices.

Chopped Egg and Onions

2 onions
8 hard cooked eggs
1½ teaspoons salt

¼ teaspoon freshly ground black pepper
4 tablespoons chicken fat (p.108)

1. Chop the onions very fine.
2. Add the eggs and continue chopping.
3. Add the salt, pepper, and chicken fat. Mix lightly.
4. Correct seasoning.
5. Pack into a greased ring mold and chill for four hours.

Note: To serve, unmold. Spread with sour cream and garnish with red or black caviar.

Egg and Caviar Mold

12 hard boiled eggs
1 tablespoon raw onion, grated
2-4 tablespoons mayonnaise

Salt and pepper
Sour cream
Caviar

1. Chop eggs; add onion, salt and pepper to taste and sufficient mayonnaise to hold together.
2. Pack into greased mold. Chill several hours or overnight.

Note: To serve, unmold. Ice with sour cream and garnish with red or black caviar.

Easy when you have the dough

You can bank on your guests' high interest rate as they delight in pizzas, patty shells and other delectibles.

3

Convenience Foods

Do rolling pins and floured boards strike terror to your heart? If kneading dough and sticky fingers are not your bag, you still can dazzle your guests with marvelous little flaky treats, thanks to today's convience foods. Straight from your supermarket shelves, these prepared doughs are easy to handle, and take just minutes to fill and bake with whatever choice morsels you desire.

Sardines in Blankets

8 canapes

1 4-ounce can small sardines in mustard sauce

1 8-ounce can crescent dinner rolls

1. Drain sardines on paper towels; reserve mustard sauce.
2. Unroll dough. Break apart on perforations into 8 triangles.
3. Brush each triangle with mustard sauce.
4. Place a sardine on wide end of triangle; roll up.
5. Place on greased baking sheet, seam side down.
6. Bake at 375° for 10-12 minutes or until dough is nicely browned.

Smoked Oyster en Croûte

1 can smoked oysters

1 can crescent rolls

1. Drain oysters.
2. Separate rolls. Cut into 1½ inch squares.
3. Place oyster in center of square. Wrap dough, sealing carefully.
4. Place on greased baking sheet.
5. Bake at 375° for 8-10 minutes or until dough is nicely browned.

The delicate smoky flavor of the smoked oyster and the crunchy texture of the flaky roll dough are a tasteful combination.

Pigs in Blankets

Thaw frozen bread dough according to directions on package. Drain Vienna sausage or cocktail weiners on paper towels. Slice in half. Wrap a small amount of dough around to cover completely. Refrigerate until one hour before serving. Let rise in warm place for 45 minutes. Bake at 350° until browned, about 10-15 minutes.

Easy Knishes

(About 36 pieces)

1 can refrigerated butterflake rolls
2 cups leftover meat (roast, steak, brisket, etc.)

1 onion
1 egg
Salt and pepper

1. Grind meat with raw onion and mix in egg, salt and pepper.
2. Separate layers of dough from rolls into small rounds (they will already be buttered). Keep roll dough *very* cold for ease in handling.
3. Place about ¾ teaspoon of meat mixture on each dough round and pinch closed.
4. Bake at 350° on cookie sheet until light brown (about 8 to 10 minutes). Serve hot.

Can be frozen on cookie sheet (before baking) and then bagged to store in freezer. To serve, thaw and then bake as above.

Miniature Meat Turnovers

Makes 32 turnovers

1 envelope Lipton Beef Flavor Mushroom Soup Mix
½ pound ground beef
1 cup drained bean sprouts

½ cup sliced water chestnuts
2 tablespoons chopped onion
2 packages refrigerator crescent rolls

1. In medium skillet, combine first five ingredients; brown well.
2. Separate crescent dough as package directs; cut in half. Place spoonful of mixture in center of each triangle; fold over and seal edges.
3. Place on ungreased cookie sheet; bake at 375° for 15 minutes or until golden.

This recipe is one of Lipton's own perennial favorites, good in taste and texture.

Hamburger Pinwheels

Serves 8

1 small onion, minced
1 pound ground beef
1 teaspoon salt

⅛ teaspoon pepper
¼ teaspoon Worcestershire
1 package refrigerator biscuits

1. Cook onion in small amount of fat until tender but not brown. Add meat and cook until browned. Drain off fat.
2. Season with salt, pepper and Worcestershire.
3. Roll out biscuit dough into a rectangle ¼ inch thick. Spread meat on dough and roll like a jelly roll.
4. Cut into slices about 1½ inches thick. Place on greased baking sheet and bake in 400° oven about 15 minutes.

Cheese and Artichoke Appetizers

4 baked patty shells
2 3-ounce packages cream cheese
  with chives
3 drops Tabasco

2 tablespoons soft butter
1 egg
6 drops Worcestershire
4 canned artichoke hearts (drained)

1. Place patty shells on an ovenproof serving dish.
2. Beat cheese with butter, egg and seasoning.
3. Place spoonful of cheese mixture in bottom of each patty shell, set an artichoke heart in the center and cover with remaining cheese.
4. Bake for about 30 minutes in the upper third of a pre-heated 475° oven until the cheese filling has puffed slightly and browned on top.

Note: An elegant first course for a dinner party; also nice when friends stop in for cocktails.

Blintz Soufflé

Serves 6

¼ cup butter or margarine
3 eggs
1 cup sour cream

Pinch of salt
*1 package frozen cheese blintzes

1. Melt shortening in casserole. Place six frozen blintzes in casserole.
2. Blend remaining ingredients and pour over blintzes.
3. Bake 1 hour at 350°.

*To make your own blintzes, see page 142 in BEGINNING AGAIN.

Instant Pizza

3 boxes English muffins
2 4-ounce cans tomato sauce
1 8-ounce package Mozzarella

2 sticks pepperoni
Parmesan cheese
Oregano

1. Slice muffins in half.
2. Spread each piece with tomato sauce.
3. Sprinkle with oregano and Parmesan cheese.
4. Put four thin slices of pepperoni on each half and cut the halves in half again if smaller servings are wanted.
5. Put thin slices of mozzarella cheese on top.
6. Place on cookie sheet.
7. Bake in a very hot oven until cheese bubbles, about 10 minutes.

Pizza

1 15-ounce can tomato sauce with tomato bits
1 8-ounce package shredded mozzarella
⅛ teaspoon oregano
1 4-ounce can sliced mushrooms, drained
1 pound bacon, chopped, fried and drained
1 tablespoon olive oil
Salt, pepper
2 tablespoons grated Parmesan
½ loaf frozen bread dough

1. Thaw loaf of frozen bread dough. Roll ½ loaf into thin circle to fit 15 inch pizza pan.
2. Grease pan. Place circle of dough into pan. Brush dough with oil.
3. Spread cheese over dough. Pour tomato sauce on cheese. Sprinkle with seasonings.
4. Spread mushrooms and bacon over pizza*. Sprinkle with olive oil and then Parmesan.
5. Bake on lowest shelf of oven at 425° for 20 minutes or until crust is browned on bottom.

Cut into squares for hors d'oeuvres. Keep hot on electric tray. This pizza may be baked, cooled completely, wrapped airtight and frozen for future use. Bake at 400° to thaw pizza and crisp crust.

*Olives, green peppers, sausage, meatballs may be used in addition to or instead of bacon and mushrooms.

Mushroom and Cream Cheese Logs

Makes 16 pieces

3 ounces chopped mushrooms
¼ teaspoon seasoned salt
1 8-ounce package refrigerator crescent rolls
1 3-ounce package cream cheese
1 beaten egg
Poppy seeds (optional)

1. Mince mushrooms. Blend well with softened cream cheese and salt.
2. Divide filling among the four rectangles of the crescent roll package and spread to cover.
3. Roll up, starting at long sides. Cut in 1½ inch pieces.
4. Brush with beaten egg and sprinkle with poppy seeds.
5. Bake on ungreased baking sheet in 375° oven for about 12 minutes. Remove to rack.

Can be prepared a few hours ahead and left refrigerated until time to bake. Keep hot on electric tray.

Note: Canned mushrooms are good, but sautéed fresh mushrooms are even better.

Arnipita
Greek Lamb Pastries

Makes 8 rolls or 32 pieces

1 pound lean ground lamb
½ pound lean ground beef
2 tablespoons tomato paste
2 tablespoons dehydrated onions
½ cup pistachio nuts or pine nuts

2 eggs
¼ teaspoon seasoned salt
Olive oil
8 sheets phyllo pastry (12x16)

1. Sauté ground meats, mixing with a fork until browned and well separated.
2. Drain excess fat.
3. Add tomato paste, seasoned salt, onions and chopped nuts.
4. Cool a few minutes and stir in beaten eggs.
5. Thaw phyllo pastry according to directions on package. Unroll and remove one sheet of pastry.
6. Lay the sheet of pastry on a tea towel. Brush half with olive oil, as in diagram A. Fold on line shown. (You will now have an 8″ by 12″ rectangle.)
7. Brush surface with olive oil. Spread ⅓ cup filling on area shown in diagram B.
8. Fold in long sides 1½ inches on dotted lines of diagram B to hold filling inside of roll.
9. Form into roll by raising towel at filled end of pastry. This will start it forming into a tight roll.
10. Place on greased pan, seam side down. Brush with a little olive oil.
11. Bake at 400° for 15-18 minutes or until browned. Drain on wire rack for 5 minutes. Serve warm. Slice into 4 pieces.

May be made ahead through step 10, covered, and refrigerated until ready to bake or baked, frozen and reheated at 350° until well warmed. Keep hot on electric tray.

Delicious, crisp and spicy—a delicate crust.

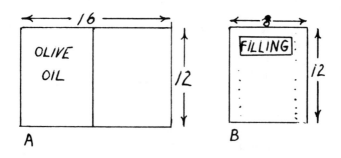

Hot Pick Ups

Watch the magic as tray after tray of rumaki, canapés and other treats disappear before your eyes.

4

Pirogen
Pastry

1½ cups sifted flour
½ teaspoon salt
½ teaspoon baking powder

½ cup shortening
1 egg, beaten
2 tablespoons cold water

1. Sift the flour, salt, and baking powder into a bowl.
2. Cut in the shortening with a pastry blender or 2 knives.
3. Add the egg and cold water, tossing lightly until a ball of dough is formed.
4. Chill while preparing the filling.

Mushroom Filling for Pirogen

3 tablespoons shortening
1 pound mushrooms, chopped
2 onions, chopped
2 tablespoons chopped parsley
1 tablespoon chopped dill

2 hard cooked egg yolks, mashed
1½ teaspoon salt
¼ teaspoon freshly ground black pepper
½ cup bread crumbs
2 tablespoons sour cream (optional)

1. Melt the shortening in a skillet.
2. Add the mushrooms and onions. Sauté for 10 minutes, or until the mushroom liquid is evaporated.
3. Add the parsley, dill, egg yolks, salt, pepper, bread crumbs, and sour cream. Mix well.
4. Preheat oven to 375°.
5. Roll the dough ⅛ inch thick on a lightly floured surface.
6. Cut into 3 inch circles.
7. Place a tablespoon of mushroom filling on each. Fold the dough over the filling, sealing the edges well.
8. Place on a greased baking sheet. Bake for 20 minutes, or until browned.

Miniature Reuben

1 package small party rye bread
Corned beef
Russian dressing

Sauerkraut, well drained
Processed Swiss cheese slices cut in 4 squares

1. Spread a little Russian dressing on one side rye bread slice.
2. Place a piece of corned beef on bread. Place a small amount of sauerkraut on corned beef and top with square of cheese.
3. Bake in 350° oven until cheese melts.

Party Turnovers

Pastry
⅓ cup shortening (half butter, half vegetable shortening)
¾ cup flour
Pinch salt
2-3 tablespoons cold water

Fillings
1 cup ground salami and
½ teaspoon horseradish or
1 cup ground chicken
¼ teaspoon curry powder
¼ teaspoon salt
3 tablespoons minced fresh parsley or 1 tablespoon dehydrated parsley

1. Make pastry by cutting in together the shortening, flour and salt. Add water, 1 tablespoon at a time, using only enough to make dough hold together. Form into ball. Chill ½ hour.
2. Roll pastry ⅛-inch thick. Cut into 2-inch squares.
3. Put 1 teaspoon of filling mixture in center of square. Fold into a triangle. Press edges together with fork.

When ready to serve, fry in hot fat (320°) for four minutes. Drain on paper towel.

Serve immediately or keep hot on electric hot tray.

Hot Potato

Serves 6

18 small unpeeled new potatoes
4 strips of crisp crumbled bacon
¼ pound butter, softened

1 clove garlic, minced
1 tablespoon parsley, chopped
Salt and pepper to taste

1. Bake potatoes (grease and pierce first) or if desired, boil instead.
2. Combine remaining ingredients.

Serve potatoes and sauce in separate bowls; sauce should be at room temperature. Make sauce ahead and refrigerate.

Men love it. Fattening but good!

This is a good sauce for potatoes served for a buffet supper.

Fried Wontons

10-15 wontons

Wonton Wrappers

1 cup flour

1 egg

½ teaspoon salt

⅓ cup water

1. Mix ingredients in a bowl and knead until very smooth, about 5 minutes.
2. Cover with a damp cloth and let rest 15-30 minutes.
3. Remove a portion of the dough to a board lightly sprinkled with cornstarch.
4. Roll dough, turning frequently until very thin.
5. Cut into 3-4 inch squares.
6. Continue until all dough is used.

Freeze if not using right away. Thaw one hour before using.

Wonton Filling

8 ounces ground pork or beef

1 egg

2 tablespoons chopped green onion
(including green tops)

1 tablespoon soy sauce

1 teaspoon salt

Dash of pepper

*½ teaspoon sesame oil

Vegetable oil

1. If using pork, brown first in skillet. Drain.
2. Place meat in a bowl and add egg, onions, salt, soy sauce and pepper. Mix well.
3. Let stand for 20 to 30 minutes.
4. Add sesame oil. It is important to add this ingredient only just before filling wrappers.
5. Place about 1 teaspoon filling in center of each square of wrapper. Fold corner to corner to make a triangle. Pinch together the widest two outer corners, so that the filled wonton folds up. Moisten edges with water to seal.
6. Heat vegetable oil in a pan to 350° and fry wontons until golden brown, about 2 minutes.

Serve hot with ginger sauce for dipping. These filled wontons can be frozen after frying. To reheat for serving, preheat oven to 400°. Turn down to 300° and heat frozen wontons for 5 minutes or until heated through.

Sesame oil is available in oriental grocery stores.

Ginger Sauce for Wontons

1 tablespoon sugar
1 tablespoon white vinegar
Dash of salt
⅓ cup water

1 tablespoon tomato catsup
1 teaspoon cornstarch
1 teaspoon freshly chopped ginger
   root

1. Boil water.
2. Add sugar, salt, catsup and vinegar. Remove from heat.
3. Stir in cornstarch and add ginger.

This sauce can be served warm or cooled. It may be made ahead and refrigerated. This will give it a spicier taste.

The Wonton wrappers may be purchased frozen.

This recipe is taught by Dora Ang in her popular oriental cooking classes in Cincinnati.

Foo Young Fritters

Makes about 48

6 eggs
*1 cup self-rising flour
1 can bean sprouts, well-drained
1 cup cooked chicken, chopped (or
   tuna fish)

1 tablespoon soy sauce
½ teaspoon Worcestershire
1 envelope onion soup mix
1 4-ounce can mushroom pieces,
   drained
1 can water chestnuts, sliced

1. Beat eggs slightly.
2. Blend in flour, soy sauce, Worcestershire until smooth. Stir in remaining ingredients.
3. Drop by teaspoonsful into hot oil. Fry at 350° for a few minutes until golden brown.
4. Drain on paper towel.

*To substitute all-purpose flour, use 1 cup flour, 1½ teaspoons baking powder and ¼ teaspoon salt.

Fish Patties

1 6-ounce can tuna or salmon,
   drained or any leftover fish
1 large potato, cooked and mashed
1 small onion, fried and cut into
   fine bits

1 egg
Salt and pepper, to taste
Dash of catsup
Bread crumbs

1. Mix all ingredients together.
2. Form into small patties, (size of a quarter). Dip in bread crumbs.
3. Fry to a light brown color.

Note: Serve patties dry or with a can of undiluted mushroom soup, or a sauce.

Breaded Artichoke Hearts
Italian Style

2 cans artichoke hearts
1 8-ounce bottle Italian dressing
¼ cup grated Romano cheese

1½ cups Italian-flavored bread
crumbs

1. Drain artichoke hearts and slice into halves or quarters.
2. Marinate in Italian dressing for 8 hours, then drain.
3. Place bread crumbs and cheese in a bag. Add artichoke hearts and shake in bag until well coated.
4. Spread on baking sheet and bake 12 to 15 minutes at 375°.

Note: A delectable Roman valentine, if you have the heart!

Artichoke Bubbles

16 slices small party rye bread
1 14-ounce can artichoke hearts, drained
1 egg white
2 tablespoons grated Parmesan

1 tablespoon mayonnaise
1 tablespoon shredded cheddar
Dash cayenne pepper
Paprika

1. Place bread slices on baking sheet. Cut artichoke hearts in half; place one half, cut side down, on each slice of bread.
2. Beat egg white until stiff. Fold in remaining ingredients except paprika. Spread on bread.
3. Top each heart with one half teaspoon of egg white mixture. Sprinkle with paprika.
4. Bake 10-15 minutes until golden brown at 400°.

Stuffed Artichoke Bottoms

20 artichoke bottoms
1 small can chopped black olives

¼ cup grated onion
¾ cup grated cheddar
4 tablespoons mayonnaise

1. Cook artichoke bottoms according to directions on package. Drain.
2. Combine remaining ingredients and stuff cavity of artichokes.
3. Preheat oven to 350°. Place artichokes on cookie sheet and bake 10 minutes or until cheese is bubbling.

Note: As a variation, use this stuffing for raw mushrooms and broil 3-5 minutes.

May be prepared through step 2 and baked when ready to serve.

Artichoke Clam Puffs

Makes about 36 pieces

2 packages frozen artichoke hearts
¼ teaspoon hot pepper sauce
1 6½-ounce can minced clams, drained

1 8-ounce package cream cheese
2 tablespoons sherry
Paprika

1. Cook artichokes according to package directions (do no overcook). Drain.
2. Beat cream cheese with pepper sauce and sherry, then stir in clams.
3. Spoon mixture onto cut side of the artichokes and sprinkle with paprika.
4. Broil until browned.

Canned artichoke bottoms may be substituted.

Curried Eggs

Serves 4

6 hard boiled eggs
Mayonnaise
Curry powder, to taste
2 tablespoons butter

2 tablespoons flour
1 cup milk
½ teaspoon Worcestershire
Salt and pepper, to taste

1. Peel eggs and remove yolks. Mash yolks with enough mayonnaise and curry powder to make a good consistency.
2. Stuff yolk mixture back into whites. Put them in a shallow casserole.
3. Make a cream sauce from remaining ingredients.
4. Pour over eggs and bake at 350° for 15 minutes.

Hot Asparagus Canapés

For each canapé:
1 thin frozen slice white bread
1 thin slice prosciutto

1 stalk canned asparagus, drained
Butter
Parmesan cheese

1. Remove crusts from white bread. Roll each slice flat between two sheets of waxed paper.
2. Spread frozen bread with softened butter. Sprinkle with Parmesan.
3. Thaw bread; place prosciutto and asparagus on corner of bread. Roll and fasten with toothpick. Brush with melted butter. Sprinkle with Parmesan.
4. Bake 10-12 minutes at 400°.

Do ahead and freeze; keeps for months if well wrapped. These can be prepared through Step 3, and refrigerated or frozen until baking.

Toasted Mushroom Rolls

Makes 3½ dozen canapés

½ pound mushrooms, finely chopped
3 tablespoons flour
¼ teaspoon MSG (optional)
2 teaspoons minced chives
1 large loaf sliced fresh white bread (20 or 24 ounce size)

¼ cup butter or margarine
¾ teaspoon salt
1 cup light cream or milk
1 teaspoon lemon juice

1. Sauté mushrooms in shortening.
2. Blend in flour, salt and MSG.
3. Stir in cream or milk. Cook until thick.
4. Add chives, lemon juice. Cool.
5. Remove crusts from slices of bread. Roll thin.
6. Spread with mixture. Roll up.
7. Pack and freeze if desired.
8. To serve, defrost, cut each roll in half and toast on all sides in 400° oven.

Note: For a more elegant and expensive dish, add 1 pound lobster meat, minced, to the mushroom mixture. Follow directions for bread using 2 regular loaves. Proceed as above. Makes about 6 dozen luscious canapés.

Refrigerator Cheese Rolls

Makes 3 dozen canapés

½ pound aged cheddar
1 tablespoon soft butter
½ teaspoon garlic salt

3 tablespoons mayonnaise
2 teaspoons Worcestershire
1 16-ounce loaf white bread, sliced

1. Grate cheese, add next four ingredients.
2. Remove crusts from slices of white bread. Roll thin.
3. Spread cheese mixture on bread and roll up.
4. Refrigerate or freeze.
5. To serve, return to room temperature and slice each roll in half. Broil until lightly browned.

Crispy Cheese Rolls

Makes about 4 dozen canapés

½ pound crock sharp cheese
½ pound Muenster cheese
¼ pound bleu cheese
1 tablespoon butter

2 eggs
1 1-pound loaf sliced bread
½ pound melted butter
½ pound chopped nuts

1. Blend bleu cheese, sharp cheese and butter in an electric mixer. Add softened Muenster and beat until smooth. Add eggs and beat until mixture is well blended.
2. Cut crusts off bread slices. Roll out very thin with rolling pin.
3. Spread with cheese and roll up like a jelly roll. Cut each roll in half.
4. Brush with melted butter. Roll in nuts.
5. Place on baking sheet, seam side down.
6. Bake 5 mintues at 450°.

These tangy crisp canapés can be prepared through step 5 in advance and frozen for future use. When frozen solid remove from baking sheet, place in airtight plastic bags and return to freezer. Remove and bake in small quantities as needed.

Emergency Canapé

Ritz crackers
Processed American cheese
Catsup or chili sauce

1. Place a small square of cheese on cracker with a dot of catsup or chili sauce in middle.
2. Broil until cheese melts a bit.

Great for unexpected guests.

Corned Beef Hash Canapés

1 can corned beef hash
1 small jar pickle slices
Durkee's dressing

Bread (preferably thin) with crusts
removed

1. Cut bread in rounds with small glass or cookie cutter.
2. Spread on Durkee's dressing.
3. Press down a pickle slice on top.
4. Make a meat ball of rounded teaspoon of hash.
5. Press meatball on top of pickle.
6. Bake at 400° until meat is well heated and bread is toasted (about 8 to 10 minutes).

These can be made ahead and frozen.

Deviled Ham Puffs

Serves 8

1 8-ounce package cream cheese
½ teaspoon baking powder
1 teaspoon milk
1 egg yolk

2 2¼-ounce cans deviled ham
30 to 35 small rounds of white
bread

1. Blend cheese, baking powder, milk and egg yolk together.
2. Toast bread on one side.
3. Spread untoasted side with deviled ham, cover with a mound of cheese mixture.
4. Bake at 375° for 10 to 12 minutes or until puffed and slightly browned.

Make ahead and bake when ready to serve.

Ham and Chutney Canapés

¼ pound ham
4 tablespoons chutney
2 tablespoons chili sauce

2 teaspoons horseradish
Toast rounds
Sliced sharp cheddar

1. Grind ham. Mix with chutney, chili sauce and horseradish.
2. Toast small rounds of bread.
3. Just before serving, spread toast rounds with ham mixture. Dot with cheese.
4. Put under broiler or bake at 475° until cheese melts.

Tuna Canapés

Makes 3 dozen canapés

3 dozen bread rounds,
1½″ to 1¼″ diameter
1 7-ounce can tuna, drained
2 tablespoons onion, finely
chopped
2 tablespoons green pepper,
chopped
1 tablespoon pimiento, chopped

¼ cup mayonnaise
¼ cup sour cream
1 teaspoon Worcestershire
2 teaspoons lemon juice
Dash of pepper
¼ cup grated American cheese
2 egg whites, stiffly beaten

1. Place bread rounds on a cookie sheet and broil until lightly browned on one side.
2. Combine tuna, onion, green pepper, pimiento, mayonnaise, sour cream, Worcestershire, lemon juice, pepper and grated cheese. Blend well.
3. Fold in stiffly beaten egg whites.
4. Top untoasted side of bread rounds with a mound of the mixture.
5. Broil about 4 inches from heat until puffed and browned. Serve immediately.

This recipe may be prepared in advance through step 2. Just before serving, continue at step 3.

Clam Puffs

Makes 24 toast rounds

1 7-ounce can minced clams
2 tablespoons heavy cream
1 3-ounce package cream cheese
¼ teaspoon dry mustard
½ teaspoon Worcestershire

¼ teaspoon salt
1 teaspoon finely minced onion
24 toast rounds
Paprika

1. Drain clams.
2. Combine clams with next six ingredients.
3. Spread on toast rounds.
4. Place under broiler until puffy.
5. Sprinkle with paprika; serve hot.

Note: Spread can be made ahead and refrigerated. Spread on toast before ready to serve.

Italian Rye Chips

½ pound grated Swiss cheese
2 tablespoons mayonnaise
Pinah rye chips

Small onion grated or onion salt to
taste

1. Mix cheese, mayonnaise and onion.
2. Put 1 teaspoon on top of each chip.
3. Broil until brown and bubbly.

*Note: Can be made ahead and refrigerated. Broil when ready to
serve. Pinah rye chips are available at specialty food shops...and
are worth the search.*

Cheese Canapés

Makes about 2 dozen small canapés

8 ounces port wine cheddar
⅓ cup chopped ripe olives
⅓ cup mayonnaise

½ teaspoon dry mustard
Freshly ground black pepper
Melba toast rounds or party rye

1. Combine all ingredients.
2. Spread on Melba toast rounds or party rye bread and heat in
   hot oven (450°) for about 5 minutes.

> **Here is the traditional cheese puff — with a difference.
> Other cheeses...other flavors. Give these variations a try.**

Cheese Puffs

1 loaf unsliced white bread
½ pound sharp cheddar
4 egg whites, stiffly beaten

2 3-ounce packages cream
cheese
1 cup butter

1. Melt cheeses and butter in double boiler.
2. When cool fold in stiffly beaten egg whites.
3. Cut crust off bread, and cut bread into 1 inch cubes, dip in
   cheese mixture; place on cookie sheet and refrigerate overnight.
4. Bake at 400° for 10 to 12 minutes. Serve warm.

Note: Can be frozen.

Swiss Sandwich Puffs

Makes 32 puffs

½ cup mayonnaise
2 tablespoons snipped
   parsley
8 slices Swiss cheese

¼ cup chopped onion
32 slices party rye

1. Combine mayonnaise, onion and parsley.
2. Spread on very lightly toasted rye slices.
3. Top each slice with ¼ of a slice of Swiss cheese.
4. Broil 2-3 minutes.

Roquefort Puffs

Makes 8 canapés

1 egg white
2 ounces Roquefort cheese spread

8 crackers or 8 2-inch bread
  rounds
Paprika

1. Beat egg white until stiff.
2. Mix cheese until creamy.
3. Fold in beaten egg white and heap on cracker or bread round.
4. Bake at 300° for 15 minutes or until brown. Garnish with
   paprika.

Toasted Cheese Rounds

½ cup mayonnaise
¼ cup Parmesan cheese, grated
Salt and pepper to taste

Very, very thin onion slices
Dash of Worcestershire
1½-inch diameter bread circles
  or rye rounds

1. Mix mayonnaise with cheese and seasonings.
2. Put one slice of onion on each circle of bread.
3. Cover onion with mayonnaise mixture. Sprinkle with additional grated Parmesan.
4. Place under broiler until brown.

Note: Can be made ahead, covered, and refrigerated until ready to broil.

Toasted Cheese Appetizers

1 8-ounce package shredded
  cheddar
1 8-ounce package shredded
  Mozzarella
Grated Parmesan to taste

Grated onion to taste, or onion
  powder
Mayonnaise
Sesame rounds

1. Mix all ingredients, adding enough mayonnaise to blend well.
2. Spread mixture on sesame rounds.
3. Place on cookie sheet and broil until cheese bubbles. This
   takes just a few minutes so watch them closely.

Easy and good for the "spur-of-the-moment" get-together. The sesame and cheese are a great combination.

CHEDDAR CHEESE PASTRY

Ha' Pennies

½ cup butter or margarine
½ pound grated sharp cheddar

½ package dry onion soup mix
1 cup flour

1. Soften shortening and cheese together at room temperature. Blend together.
2. Add onion soup mix and flour to form stiff dough.
3. Shape into rolls about 1-inch in diameter. Wrap in waxed paper and chill.
4. Cut into slices about ¼-inch thick.
5. Bake on ungreased baking sheet in 375° oven for 10 to 15 minutes. If desired, top with a pecan, almond or walnut before baking.
6. Remove from pan. Cool on wire rack. Store in airtight can.

A very tasty appetizer.

Cheddar Cheese Crisps

1 pound cheddar
2 cups flour
⅞ cup margarine, softened

2 drops Tabasco
1 teaspoon Worcestershire

1. Grate cheese and mash well with the margarine. Add Tabasco and Worcestershire.
2. Stir in flour and mix well.
3. Shape into a 1-inch roll, put in foil and refrigerate several hours.
4. Remove from refrigerator, cut in ¼-inch slices, place on cookie sheets, bake 12 to 15 minutes in 350° oven until lightly browned.
5. Remove from pan. Cool on wire rack. Store in airtight can.

Can be made ahead of time, refrigerated or frozen until ready to bake.

Variations of Cheddar Cheese Pastry

(See Page 64)

Pecan Pastry

Add 1 cup chopped pecans for each cup of flour.

Marmalade Turnovers

Cut pastry into circles. Put ½ teaspoon of marmalade in center of circle, fold over edge and mash edges together with a fork. Bake at 375° for 10 minutes. Keep in covered tin. They freeze beautifully after being baked. Reheat thoroughly before serving. Makes 2 to 3 dozen.

Golden Olive Nuggets

Drain olives and pat dry. Use about 1 teaspoon dough for each olive, wrapping the olive with the dough. Roll in seeds of your choice. Bake 15 minutes in preheated 400° oven and serve while warm. Makes about 36 nuggets.

These may be frozen before baking and popped into the oven when ready to serve. Arrange on baking sheet and freeze firm. Store in plastic bag in freezer. To serve, thaw and bake as directed.

For an interesting variation, wrap cheese pastry around almond stuffed or onion stuffed olives. The canapés can be rolled in sesame seed before baking for added crunchiness and flavor.

Mushrooms Stuffed with Spinach

Serves 10

1 pound mushrooms
1 10-ounce package frozen spinach
½ cup butter

1 tablespoon chopped onion
Salt, pepper, nutmeg
Grated cheddar

1. Wash and drain mushrooms. Remove stems and chop.
2. Sauté onion in ½ butter. Then sauté chopped mushroom stems.
3. Remove with slotted spoon. Add remaining butter and carefully sauté mushroom caps for a short time to coat them well with butter.
4. Cook and drain spinach. Put in blender with mushroom stems, onion and seasoning. Purée.
5. Fill mushroom caps with mixture. Sprinkle with grated cheese.
6. Bake at 375° for 15 minutes.

Note: If large mushroom caps are used they make a nice vegetable garnish for steak dinner.

Stuffed Mushrooms

Serves 6

24 large mushrooms
3 tablespoons low calorie cream cheese
1 tablespoon butter
3 green onions

Salt and pepper
1 tablespoon seasoned bread crumbs
Milk

1. Clean mushroom caps and dry.
2. Chop mushroom stems and sauté with cut-up green onions, salt, and pepper in butter.
3. Remove from heat and add crumbs and cream cheese to mushroom mixture.
4. Stuff mushroom caps and place in baking dish that has thin layer of milk in it so mushrooms will not stick.
5. Bake 15 minutes at 350°.

Make ahead and refrigerate until baking time.

Mushrooms - All Puffed Up

1 pound fresh mushrooms
¼ cup butter
¼ cup chopped onion
Bread rounds - 2 inches in
    diameter as many as there are
    mushrooms

Salt, pepper, pinch of sugar
1 cup bleu cheese, crumbled
2 eggs, beaten

1. Clean mushrooms. Remove stems. Drain caps and stems.
2. Sauté mushroom caps in butter about two minutes. Set aside to cool.
3. Chop stems and sauté with onions in butter. Add seasonings. Mix well.
4. Spread chopped mixture on bread rounds.
5. Mix eggs and cheese. Form into balls to fit inside mushroom caps.
6. Fill caps with cheese balls. Put filled mushrooms on toast rounds.
7. Broil 3-4 inches from heat — 7-10 minutes — or until cheese is lightly browned and puffy.

Can be made ahead and broiled at the last minute.

Nashville Nosh

Mushrooms
Ground hot sausage meat

Sesame seed

1. Wash and dry mushrooms. Remove stems.
2. Roll sausage into balls. Stuff in mushroom caps.
3. Sprinkle with sesame seeds.
4. Broil or bake at 500° for 10 minutes.

Keep hot on electric tray. Insist you've been working on these all day.

Simple Stuffed Mushrooms

Large mushrooms
¼ cup butter

Deviled ham or sharp cheese
spread

1. Wash and dry mushrooms. Remove stems.
2. Melt butter in skillet. Add mushrooms in one layer. Turn when edges begin to brown (cooking should take 4-5 minutes).
3. Drain on paper toweling.
4. Fill with deviled ham or any sharp cheese spread.
5. Just before serving, heat for a few minutes in a 350° oven.

Make ahead. Refrigerate until ready to use.

Meat Filled Mushroom Caps

24 large mushrooms
½ cup soy sauce
½ pound ground beef
¼ cup minced green pepper
2 tablespoons bread crumbs

1 egg yolk
1 tablespoon minced onion
½ clove minced garlic
¼ teaspoon salt
¼ teaspoon pepper

1. Wash and drain mushrooms; remove stems.
2. Marinate caps for 1 hour in soy sauce.
3. Finely chop tender portion of stems and mix with remaining ingredients.
4. Drain caps, reserve soy sauce. Stuff with meat mixture, mounded high. Brush tops with reserved soy sauce.
5. Broil 8-10 minutes.

May be served immediately after broiling. If you wish to "do it ahead," broil; refrigerate or freeze. When ready to serve, defrost and bake at 350° for 8-10 minutes.

Mushroom Flambé

Serves 8-10

3 tablespoons butter
2 tablespoons oil
1 pound fresh mushrooms
Salt
Pepper
Tarragon

Chives
Parsley
4 tablespoons sherry
1 tablespoon lemon juice
Few grains sugar
1 jigger brandy

1. Heat butter and oil in chafing dish. Sauté mushrooms.
2. Add herbs, spices, sherry, and lemon juice. Cover and cook 3-4 minutes.
3. Add sugar, heated brandy and ignite.

Serve on toothpicks. This recipe is elegant and easy. Make it in your chafing dish.

Mushroom Puffs

Makes 35 to 40 puffs

1 4-ounce can button mushrooms
1 8-ounce package cream cheese, softened
½ small onion, minced
1 loaf of thinly sliced bread

Garlic powder
Seasoned salt
2 egg yolks
Salt, pepper

1. Cut bread into rounds 1½ inch in diameter with cookie cutter or juice glass. Place a mushroom in center.
2. Mix cream cheese with egg yolks and onions. Add rest of seasoning to taste.
3. Cover mushroom with cheese mixture.
4. Place under broiler until brown and puffy.

Cheese and Mushroom Canapés

Makes 2½ dozen

¼ pound mushrooms
1 tablespoon butter
1 8-ounce package cream cheese
Cream

1 teaspoon minced onions
Salt and pepper
Small rounds of bread
Butter for rounds of toasted bread

1. Chop mushrooms in tiny pieces. Cook for a few minutes in butter.
2. Mix mushrooms with cream cheese, salt, pepper and minced onion and enough cream to soften.
3. Toast small rounds of bread on one side.
4. Spread untoasted side with butter, then mushroom mixture. Refrigerate or freeze.
5. When ready to serve, place under broiler until puffy and brown.

Cheese Puffs

Very Easy

Will serve 10 (if other canapés will be served, too)

1 tablespoon flour
1 cup grated sharp cheese
1 teaspoon garlic salt

1 tablespoon dry sherry
2 egg whites
Crustless bread cut into quarters

1. Mix flour, garlic salt and cheese; stir in wine.
2. Beat egg whites until stiff and fold into first mixture.
3. Drop by the level tablespoon onto a cookie sheet.
4. Freeze, then transfer frozen cheese "drops" to a plastic bag for longer freezer storage.
5. To serve: place a frozen cheese ball on ¼ slice square of crustless bread, or place a frozen cheese ball on crisp cracker.
6. Arrange on a cookie sheet and heat for about 5 minutes in a 350° oven or until cheese mixture begins to bubble.

Note: For microwave oven:
Place the frozen cheese balls on crackers or bread on a 7-inch round paper plate. Heat in microwave oven for 1¾ to 2 minutes before serving.

RUMAKI

Rumaki and Other Bacon Treats

General Instructions

1. Cut bacon slices crosswise into thirds or halves depending on size of food to be wrapped. (It should overlap slightly.)
2. Secure overlapped bacon around food with a wooden toothpick.
3. These appetizers may be either baked or broiled. Broiling is slightly faster, but baking offers the advantage of less danger of burning.

   To broil: Place 3 inches from source of heat. When topside is crisp, turn and continue broiling until second side is crisp.

   To bake: Bake at 425°, until bacon is crisp. Turn once during baking.

4. Drain on paper towels.
5. Keep hot on electric tray.
6. If prepared in advance, they may be reheated in a 350° oven for 5 minutes, or until heated through.

Rumaki

Makes 16-20

1 5-ounce can water chestnuts
¼ cup soy sauce

4-5 slices bacon
Sugar

1. Drain water chestnuts. Marinate in soy sauce several hours.
2. Cut water chestnuts in half if very large. Roll in sugar.
3. Cut bacon slices in half crosswise and again lengthwise.
4. Wrap water chestnuts in bacon slices. Secure with a toothpick.
5. Bake at 425° until bacon is crisp. Turn once.
6. Drain on paper towels.

May be made the day before. Refrigerate. Before serving, reheat 10 minutes at 350°. Serve in chafing dish.

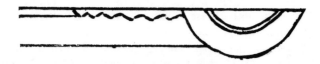

Broiled Stuffed Dates

Dates (seeds removed)   Sherry
Chopped nuts   Bacon
Cream cheese or cheddar

1. Soak dried dates in sherry at least 36 hours.
2. Split and fill with nuts or cream cheese or a combination of both, or stuff with cheddar cheese.
3. Wrap ⅓ slice bacon around fruit tightly to seal in filling and secure with toothpick.
4. Broil or bake until bacon is crisp.

Bacon Wrapped Water Chestnuts and Pineapple

Bacon slices, cut in thirds   Drained canned pineapple chunks
Water chestnut slices

1. Wrap a bacon slice around a chunk of pineapple and a slice of water chestnut and secure with a toothpick.
2. Broil or bake until bacon is crisp, turning once.
3. Drain on paper towels.
4. May be reheated on a rack in a shallow baking pan in a preheated 350° oven for 5 minutes.

Brazil Nuts in Bacon

2 tablespoons butter   Bacon strips cut in thirds
Brazil nuts   Salt

1. Melt butter in pan and sauté nuts until golden brown, remove pan from heat and salt nuts slightly.
2. Wrap bacon around nut and secure with toothpick.
3. Broil until bacon is crisp, turning often.

Artichoke Hearts and Bacon Tidbits

1 can artichoke hearts, drained   Bacon strips, cut in thirds.
Onion powder

1. Cut artichoke hearts in half and sprinkle with onion powder.
2. Wrap bacon slice around artichoke heart and secure with a toothpick.
3. Bake or broil until bacon is crisp, turning once.

Bacon Watermelon Rinds

Bacon   Watermelon rind slices

1. Wrap ½ slice of bacon around bite size pieces of watermelon rind. Fasten with toothpicks.
2. Bake at 425° until bacon is crisp. Turn once.

These tidbits can be prepared ahead and refrigerated and baked at serving time.

Stuffed Prune Broil

Makes 16

16 pitted prunes (preferably large)   16 chunks of pineapple
Sherry wine to cover prunes   8 slices of bacon

1. Soak prunes several days in sherry.
2. Stuff one chunk pineapple in each prune.
3. Stretch ½ slice bacon and wrap around prune.
4. Secure bacon with toothpick.
5. Bake at 425° until bacon is well cooked and crisp. Turn once.

Note: Unused can be frozen, and water chestnuts (split) can be subsituted for pineapple.

Bacon Wrapped Prune and Cheese Canapés

Large seedless prunes   Bacon strips
Aged cheddar   Teriyaki sauce

1. Slit open prunes.
2. Fill with cheddar cheese cubes, cut 6 to the ounce.
3. Wrap with ½ slice bacon tightly to seal in cheese. Fasten with toothpick.
4. Sprinkle with teriyaki sauce. Refrigerate several hours or overnight.
5. Bake at 425° until bacon is crisp. Turn once.

These are an instant hit. Your guest will never guess what the secret ingredients are.

Bacon Wrapped Scallops

Fresh bay or sea scallops   Bacon strips
Teriyaki sauce

1. Wash and drain scallops. Cut large ones in half.
2. Marinate scallops in teriyaki sauce several hours or overnight.
3. Wrap in ½ strip of bacon. Secure with toothpick.
4. Sprinkle with additional teriyaki sauce.
5. Bake at 425° until bacon is crisp, turning once.

Angels on Horseback

Oysters, fresh or frozen   Bacon slices, cut in half or thirds
Salt, pepper, paprika

1. Season oysters with salt, pepper and paprika.
2. Wrap bacon slice around oyster and secure with toothpick.
3. Broil or bake slowly until crisp, turning once.

Frankfurters, Cheese and Bacon

Cocktail frankfurters   Bacon strips, cut in thirds
Cheddar cheese

1. Split cocktail frankfurter and insert a piece of cheddar cheese.
2. Wrap with a slice of bacon tightly to seal in cheese and secure with a toothpick.
3. Bake at 350° for about 20 minutes, or until bacon is crisp.

Broiled Olives in Bacon

Large stuffed olives   Bacon slices, cut in halves or thirds

1. Wrap olives with bacon and secure with toothpick.
2. Broil, turning occasionally, until bacon is crisp. Drain on absorbent paper.

Blini with Sour Cream and Caviar

2 eggs
1 medium onion, quartered
1 teaspoon salt

2 cups diced raw potatoes
¼ cup parsley clusters
¼ cup flour

1. Into blender container, put eggs, onion, salt, parsley, and half of diced potatoes. Cover container and turn motor on high.
2. Uncover container, and with motor on, add flour and remaining half of potatoes. As soon as last cube of potato is added turn off motor.
3. Fry tiny pancakes (half-dollar size) in ¼ inch deep hot fat. Turn when light brown on bottom. Remove when second side is light brown.
4. Drain very well on paper towels.
5. When cold, pack on an aluminum foil tray, waxed paper between layers. Wrap for freezer.
6. At time of use, heat in 450° oven in single layer. When hot and brown, drain well on paper towels, serve with bowls of caviar and sour cream.

Pick a rainy day when you have nothing else to do. Make lots! They freeze well and will keep for several months. They can be removed from freezer in any needed quantity. Instant elegance!

Petite Potato Pancakes

2 cups raw grated potatoes
2 eggs, beaten well
1 tablespoon flour

⅛ teaspoon baking powder
½ onion, grated
Dash pepper
1½ teaspoons salt

1. Grate potatoes and drain well, pressing out excess water.
2. Add remaining ingredients and blend thoroughly.
3. Drop from tablespoon into well-greased frying pan. Brown on both sides.
4. Set aside. Reheat in 350° oven for 10 minutes.

Serve with sour cream and caviar. Makes about 30 cocktail-size pancakes.
May be made through step 3 and heated when ready to serve.

Brandeis Special

1 package small party rye bread
Thin slices kosher salami
Russian dressing

Sliced processed Swiss cheese
(cut into 4 squares)

1. Spread a little Russian dressing on one side of rye bread slice.
2. Place a slice of salami on bread and top with square of cheese.
3. Bake in 350° oven until cheese is melted and salami sizzles a little.

Cold Pick Ups

Cream puffs, deviled eggs and other chilled pretties never get the cold shoulder, but rather make for a warm reception.

5

Anchovy Canapés

Makes 20 canapé

6 tablespoons butter
2 tablespoons anchovy paste
20 bread rounds

20 arthichoke hearts
8 ounces whipped cream cheese
Pimiento

1. Blend butter and anchovy paste.
2. Spread rounds with anchovy butter.
3. Ring outer edge with cream cheese.
4. In center place artichoke heart and dot of pimiento.

Shrimp Cheese Balls

Makes about 3½ dozen

1 8-ounce package cream cheese
1½ teaspoons prepared mustard
1 teaspoon grated onion
1 teaspoon lemon juice
Dash cayenne pepper

Dash salt
1 4½-ounce can (¾ cup) shrimp,
  drained
⅔ cup chopped salted mixed nuts

1. Soften cream cheese.
2. Blend in mustard, onion, lemon juice, cayenne pepper and salt.
3. Break shrimp into pieces; stir into cheese mixture. Chill.
4. Form into ½-inch balls, and roll in chopped nuts.
5. Chill until ready to serve.

Curried Chicken Balls

Makes 5 dozen

1 8-ounce package cream cheese
4 tablespoons mayonnaise
1½ cups chopped almonds
1 tablespoon butter

2 cups chopped cooked chicken
3 tablespoons chopped chutney
1 teaspoon salt
2 teaspoons curry powder
1 cup grated coconut

1. Blend cheese and mayonnaise.
2. Sauté almonds in butter until lightly browned.
3. Add almonds, chicken, chutney, salt and curry powder to cream cheese mixture.
4. Shape into walnut sized balls. Roll each ball in coconut. Chill until ready to serve.

These can be frozen. Serve with large colored toothpicks.

Bologna Wedges

1 3-ounce package cream cheese   2 tablespoons cream
1 tablespoon horseradish   6 slices bologna

1. Combine cheese, horseradish and cream.
2. Spread on five slices of bologna. Stack together and top with one unspread slice.
3. Chill until cheese is hard. Slice into wedges for hors d'oeuvres.

Delicious with Kosher bologna.

Corned Beef Canapés

1 cucumber, chopped and drained   Corned beef, thinly sliced
1 3-ounce package cream cheese

1. Mix finely chopped cucumber with softened cream cheese.
2. Spread on small slices of corned beef.
3. Roll up tightly; wrap in waxed paper. Chill ½ hour before serving.

Also good with ham or smoked salmon.

Lox Pinwheels

4 ounces whipped cream cheese   ½ pound lox* (smoked salmon)
1 teaspoon chives   1 dozen miniature bagels, split and buttered

1. Mix cream cheese and chives.
2. Spread mixture on lox; roll up like a jelly roll.
3. Wrap tightly in waxed paper. Refrigerate at least 4 hours.
4. Slice crosswise to give a pinwheel effect.

Serve on bagel. Everything can be done in the a.m. but do not place lox mixture on bagel until last minute.

*To make your own lox, see page 114 of BEGINNING AGAIN.

Prosciutto and Asparagus

1. Drain canned asparagus, wrap a small piece of prosciutto around it.
2. Fasten with toothpick. Serve cold.

Prosciutto and Melon

1. Make 1 inch cantaloupe cubes.
2. Wrap a small piece of prosciutto around each cube. Fasten with a toothpick. Serve cold.

Cheese-Fruit Appetizers

Spear a cube of sharp cheddar cheese and a grape, mandarin orange section or a pineapple chunk with a toothpick. Walnut or pecan halves are also good with cheese.

Cheese-Nut Appetizers

1. Mash together equal quantities of butter and Roquefort or bleu cheese.
2. Spread a little of the cheese mixture between two walnut halves; chill.

Salted nuts may be used.

Deviled Cream Cheese Balls

Makes 30 balls

1 8-ounce package cream cheese
1 2¼-ounce can deviled ham

1 8-ounce can pineapple tidbits, drained
Chopped parsley or chives

1. Blend cream cheese and deviled ham. Chill.
2. Place pineapple tidbits on paper towel to drain well. Cut each piece in half crosswise.
3. Roll a spoonful of cheese mixture around each pineapple piece to form a 1-inch ball. Chill.
4. Roll in chopped parsley or chives when ready to serve.

Serve with toothpicks.

Deviled Eggs

General Directions

To boil eggs:
1. Prick one end of egg with a pin to prevent cracking.
2. Place eggs gently in saucepan, cover with cold water.
3. Bring to boil; reduce heat to keep water simmering and continue to cook for 15 minutes.
4. Pour off boiling water and let cold tap water run over eggs until cool enough to handle.
5. Remove shell and slice eggs in half. They can be sliced either lengthwise or crosswise. To make crosswise cut eggs stand on platter, trim off a small slice of egg white from rounded end.
6. Stuff eggs with filling of your choice. They may be garnished with paprika, curry powder, a slice of stuffed green olive, a slice of pimiento, a caper, a rolled anchovy, red or black caviar. Choose garnish to harmonize with filling.
7. To prepare fillings: remove egg yolks, mash and combine with all remaining ingredients except garnishes. Refill egg whites. Pastry tube can be used, if desired, for decorative effect.
8. Deviled eggs may be prepared a day or two ahead and stored in refrigerator, wrapped air tight with plastic wrap. Add garnish a few hours before serving.

Fillings

Fillings are sufficient for 12 halves unless otherwise noted.

Basic Deviled Eggs

6 egg yolks
*¼ cup mayonnaise
¼ teaspoon salt
Dash freshly ground pepper
2 teaspoons prepared mustard

1 tablespoon finely chopped celery
1 tablespoon finely chopped stuffed green olives
1 tablespoon finely chopped green onion

Pink Deviled Eggs

6 egg yolks
1 7¾-ounce can salmon, drained
*½ cup mayonnaise
1 tablespoon minced pimiento
1 teaspoon grated onion

1 teaspoon dry mustard
Salt and pepper to taste
Few drops Tabasco
Parsley for garnish

> *Note: The amount of mayonnaise will depend on the size of the eggs; add sparingly with small eggs.*

Anchovy Stuffed Eggs

6 egg yolks
1 teaspoon anchovy paste
*3 tablespoons mayonnaise
¼ teaspoon sugar

1 tablespoon finely chopped
  parsley or 1 teaspoon
  dehydrated parsley

Sardine Stuffed Eggs

6 egg yolks
1 4-ounce can boneless, skinless,
  oil packed sardines, drained

*3-4 tablespoons mayonnaise
Seasoned salt (to taste)
2 teaspoons lemon juice

Smoked Salmon Stuffed Eggs

6 egg yolks
**4 ounces smoked salmon finely
  chopped (½ cup)
*¼ cup mayonnaise
¼ teaspoon salt

Dash freshly ground pepper
1 tablespoon finely chopped
  parsley or 1 teaspoon
  dehydrated parsley
Drained black olives and pimiento
  to garnish

Deviled Ham and Eggs

6 egg yolks
1 2¼-ounce can deviled ham
¼ teaspoon Worcestershire
1 tablespoon prepared mustard

3 drops onion juice
*1-3 tablespoons mayonnaise
  (enough to moisten)
Salt
White pepper

Crabmeat Eggs

Makes 24 halves

12 egg yolks
1 cup crabmeat
½ cup minced celery
½ cup chopped almonds

2 tablespoons minced green pepper
*Mayonnaise to moisten
1 teaspoon prepared mustard
¼ teaspoon salt

Note: May be made with tuna fish. The crunchy texture of almonds and the tasty crabmeat will surprise and delight your guests.

*See note page 79.

**To make your own smoked salmon, see page 114 in* BEGINNING AGAIN.

Chicken Stuffed Eggs

6 egg yolks
½ cup minced chicken breast
¼ cup chopped celery
1 teaspoon prepared mustard
1-2 tablespoons sour cream

*2 tablespoons mayonnaise
2 tablespoons chopped pistachio
  nuts
Salt and pepper to taste
Paprika to garnish

Chicken Deviled Eggs

6 egg yolks
½ cup minced chicken or turkey
4 drops onion juice
1 teaspoon anchovy paste

3 drops lemon juice
*1-3 tablespoons mayonnaise
Salt and pepper

Garnish with rolled anchovy fillet (with caper in center).

Chutney Eggs

6 egg yolks
3 slices crisp cooked, crumbled
  bacon

*1-2 tablespoons mayonnaise
3 tablespoons finely chopped
  chutney, drained

Deviled Eggs
Low Calorie

6 warm, hard cooked egg yolks
¼ teaspoon salt
¼ teaspoon dry mustard

¼ cup plain yogurt
½ teaspoon Worcestershire
1 teaspoon lemon juice
Parsley

Mushroom Stuffed Eggs Russian Style

8 eggs
1 4-ounce can mushrooms
1 small onion, minced
2 teaspoons butter
2 tablespoons mayonnaise

4 teaspoons sour cream
Salt, pepper to taste
Pinch cayenne
Pimiento
Parsley

1. Slice cooled hard boiled eggs in half and remove yolks and mash.
2. In melted butter, fry onion and chopped mushrooms.
3. Mix onion-mushroom mixture with mashed egg yolks and season with salt, pepper and cayenne. If necessary, add a little mayonnaise to bind mixture.
4. Stuff egg whites, mounding the filling.
5. Mix mayonnaise and sour cream together and spoon onto stuffed eggs.
6. Garnish with pimiento pieces and chopped parsley.

*See note page 79.

Duchesses
Tiny Cream Puffs

½ cup butter
⅛ teaspoon salt
1 cup boiling water

1 cup sifted flour
3 eggs

1. Add butter and salt to boiling water and stir over medium heat until mixture boils.
2. Reduce heat, add flour all at once and beat vigorously until mixture leaves the sides of pan.
3. Remove from heat and add 1 egg at a time, beating thoroughly after each addition.
4. Shape puffs, using about 1 teaspoon paste for each one.
5. On greased cookie sheet bake in a 450° oven for about 8 minutes or until points begin to brown, then reduce heat to 350° and continue baking 10 to 12 minutes longer. Cool on wire rack.
6. When cold, cut tops from duchesses, fill lower half and press top over filling.

Fillings For Cream Puffs

Cream Cheese and Ham

2 3-ounce packages cream cheese, softened

1 2¼-ounce deviled ham
Catsup to moisten.

Blend well.

Cream Cheese and Roquefort

1 3-ounce package cream cheese
Roquefort cheese to taste

Dry sherry to moisten

Blend well.

Additional Fillings

Chopped chicken salad, tuna fish or egg salad or any favorite spread filling.

Meaty Subjects

This chapter is the "meating" place filled with everything from meatballs to chicken liver. Each bite is small but mighty — mighty good, that is.

6

MEATBALLS

In miniature the meatball is an easy, inexpensive, do-it-ahead hors d'oeuvre. For a main course shape larger meatballs.

Miniature Stuffed Cabbages

2 small cabbages
1 cup chopped onion
1 clove garlic, sliced
2 15-ounce cans tomato sauce with tomato bits
2 cups water
Juice of 3 lemons
⅔ cup brown sugar

½ cup raisins
1 cup cooked rice (⅓ cup raw)
1½ pounds ground round
¼ cup grated onion
1 teaspoon salt
⅛ teaspoon pepper
½-¾ cup ginger snaps, crumbled

1. Select small firm cabbages and boil until leaves become flexible enough to separate and roll. Set aside to cool.
2. In a large, heavy skillet sauté onions and garlic. Add tomato sauce, water, lemon juice, brown sugar, raisins and salt and pepper to taste.
3. While sauce is cooking, prepare rice. Add raw ground round to cooked rice; add grated onion, salt and pepper to raw meat mixture.
4. Separate cabbage leaves. Trim the base of the leaf with a vegetable peeler to the same thickness as rest of leaf.
5. Roll meat-rice mixture into cabbage leaves (make small). Secure with good quality wood toothpicks.
6. Place carefully into tomato sauce mixture and cook slowly for 2 or 3 hours in a covered pan.
7. Mix ginger snaps with ¾ cup sauce. Add to remaining sauce during last ½ hour. Stir occasionally to prevent burning or sticking.

Better made day ahead and refrigerated overnight. Can be reheated in casserole dish in oven.

Russian Meatballs

1 cup diced onion
2 tablespoons shortening
2 slices white bread
1 pound ground chuck
½ cup catsup or more as needed

1 egg
1 teaspoon salt
¼ teaspoon paprika
⅛ teaspoon lemon pepper

1. Sauté onions in shortening. Place in casserole.
2. Make crumbs out of bread and add to meat. Mix with 2 tablespoons catsup, egg, salt, paprika, and lemon pepper.
3. Shape into 20 meatballs. Place on top of onions, sprinkle with additional salt, lemon pepper, paprika and remaining catsup. Simmer covered on low heat 1½ hours.

Meatballs Stroganoff

½ cup chopped onion
1 tablespoon butter
½ pound sliced mushrooms
1 pound lean ground round
1 teaspoon salt
¼ teaspoon pepper
½ cup bread crumbs
⅓ cup water

3 ounces tomato paste
3 tablespoons bouillon
½ cup sherry
1 tablespoon Worcestershire
1½ teaspoons celery salt
¼ cup sliced green pepper
1 tablespoon caraway seed
1 cup sour cream

1. Sauté onion in butter. Set aside.
2. Sauté mushrooms in butter. Set aside.
3. Mix ground round, salt, pepper, bread crumbs, and water. Form into small meatballs.
4. Sauté meatballs until lightly browned or place on baking pan in 500° oven for 6-8 minutes.
5. Combine meatballs, onion, tomato paste, bouillon, sherry, Worcestershire and celery salt. Simmer 20 minutes.
6. Add caraway seed and green pepper and simmer 10 minutes longer. Stir in sour cream and mushrooms and heat just to boiling point. (Do not boil sour cream or it will curdle.)

An inexpensive version of a gourmet recipe which usually uses steak as the meat. Keep hot in chafing dish.

To prepare in advance: Finish through step 5. Freeze or refrigerate 1-3 days. Thaw; heat to boiling. Resume directions at step 6.

Meatballs in Potato Dill Sauce

Serves 4-6

2 slices white bread, cubed
1½ cups milk
1 pound ground chuck
1 egg
2 tablespoons parsley
1 teaspoon salt

¼ teaspoon pepper
2 tablespoons salad oil
2 10½-ounce cans condensed
    cream of potato soup
3 tablespoons dill weed

1. In medium bowl, place bread. Add ½ cup milk and let stand until milk is absorbed.
2. Stir in chuck, egg, parsley, and salt and pepper.
3. Shape into 1 inch balls. Brown in oil and drain on paper towels.
4. Meanwhile, in medium sauce pan over medium heat, heat undiluted soup, remaining cup of milk, and dill weed until boiling. Add meatballs and heat through.

Make ahead. Refrigerate or freeze. Reheat. Serve in chafing dish.

Chinese Meatballs

Makes 3 dozen

Meatballs
1 pound ground beef
1 egg
1 teaspoon salt
2 tablespoons chopped onion
Pepper
½ cup bread crumbs
¼ cup water

Sauce
3 tablespoons cornstarch
1 tablespoon soy sauce
3 tablespoons vinegar
½ cup sugar
1 tablespoon oil
1½ cups pineapple juice
4 slices pineapple
1 green pepper
1 jar sliced pimiento

1. Mix together ingredients for meatballs.
2. Form into 36 small balls. Bake at 375° for 10 minutes, un-covered.
3. Mix cornstarch with soy sauce, vinegar, ¼ cup pineapple juice and sugar. Blend well to remove lumps. Add oil and remaining pineapple juice. Bring to boil, stirring frequently and cook 1 minute.
4. Cut pineapple and green pepper into chunks and add to sauce.
5. Add meatballs. Heat until meatballs are warmed through.

A great do it ahead recipe!
Meatballs may be baked and frozen ahead. Sauce may be made ahead, but add pinepple, green pepper and pimiento at time of reheating. Serve piping hot in chafing dish.

As a main course, add ½ cup sliced water chestnuts and 1 cup pea pods. Serve over rice. Meatballs may be larger in size.

Goody Meatballs from the Chafing Dish

Meatballs
3 pounds ground beef (round if you can afford it)
2 cups Parmesan cheese, grated
5 eggs
2 teaspoons salt
⅛ teaspoon pepper
4 cloves garlic, minced
6 slices white bread, soaked and squeezed
Enough olive oil to cover bottom of pan

Sauce
2½ bottles of catsup (14 ounces each)
2½ cups white wine

1. Mix meat, cheese, eggs, salt, pepper, garlic and bread.
2. Form meatballs (larger than a marble but smaller than a golf ball). Brown carefully in olive oil.
3. Make sauce of catsup and wine.
4. Simmer meatballs in sauce 10 minutes in chafing dish.

Make ahead. Refrigerate or freeze. Warm and serve in chafing dish with toothpicks.

Dolmadakia Avgolemono
Stuffed grape leaves with lemon sauce

½ pound lean ground lamb
½ pound lean ground beef
1 teaspoon salt
½ teaspoon basil
2 tablespoons dehydrated onion
¼ teaspoon freshly ground pepper
¼ cup raw rice
2 teaspoons dill weed
1 tablespoon dehydrated parsley
1 egg

1 jar grape leaves
2 cups chicken broth
½ cup dry white wine
6 tablespoons lemon juice
Whole rind of lemon
1 clove garlic
1 stick cinnamon
4 egg yolks
1-2 teaspoons Wondra flour to
   thicken

1. Mix beef, lamb, salt, basil, onion, pepper, rice, dill weed, parsley and egg until well blended.
2. Rinse grape leaves. Drain on paper towels.
3. Place 1 tablespoon meat in center of each leaf. Roll from stem end, tucking in edges to hold meat in place. Secure with a wooden toothpick.
4. Mix broth, wine, 3 tablespoons of lemon juice, lemon rind, garlic and cinnamon stick in pot. Place a layer of grape leaves in pot. Lay meat rolls in layers. Simmer for 1 hour, basting occasionally with sauce. Add more broth if necessary during cooking.
5. Remove rolls from broth; reserve broth. Place in bake and serve dish for reheating.
6. Strain broth, discarding lemon peel, garlic and cinnamon. Beat egg yolks and remaining 3 tablespoons lemon juice. Beat in hot broth. Cook in double boiler until thick, stirring frequently with wire whisk.

A piquant, easily prepared dish. Delicious!
To serve: Cover meat rolls and heat in 300° oven until very hot. (They may be refrigerated or frozen and reheated.)

The sauce is best reheated over boiling water to prevent curdling and separating. It may be frozen but it should be stirred with a wire whisk when reheating.

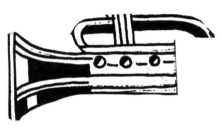

Sweet and Sour Meatballs

½ cup water
⅓ cup packed dark brown sugar
¼ cup lemon juice
1 tablespoon catsup
¾ pound ground round steak

1 egg
¼ cup bread crumbs
¼ teaspoon salt
Dash pepper

1. Combine water, brown sugar, lemon juice and catsup in saucepan. Heat to boiling.
2. In medium bowl, combine ground round, egg, bread crumbs, salt and pepper. Form into meatballs. Place in saucepan.
3. Cook, covered over low heat for 15 minutes.

Can be made ahead and frozen. Serve in chafing dish with toothpicks.

Meatballs and Cocktail Onions

½ pound lean ground round
1 tablespoon grated Parmesan
   cheese
1 tablespoon catsup

¾ teaspoon salt
Dash pepper
Cocktail onions

1. Mix meat and seasonings.
2. Drain onions.
3. Make meat into balls with onions in center. Chill.
4. Bake at 450° for 5 minutes.

Best rare.

Swedish Meatballs

Serves 8 to 10

Meatballs
2 pounds ground chuck
2 eggs
1 tablespoon minced onion
1 tablespoon milk

Sauce
1 10-ounce can jellied cranberry
 sauce
1 bottle chili sauce
1 cup water
1 10-ounce can sauerkraut

1. Combine meat, eggs, onion and milk. Make into small balls.
2. Mix cranberry sauce, chili sauce, water and drained sauerkraut.
3. Place layers of meatballs and sauce in casserole. Bake at 325° for 45 minutes. Stir once after 25 minutes.

Make ahead; refrigerate. Reheat and serve in chafing dish.

Meatballs Elmira

Meatballs
2 pounds ground beef
½ cup milk
2 small onions, grated
2 eggs
½ teaspoon pepper
4 slices white bread
2 tablespoons minced parsley
1 teaspoon salt

Sauce
8 ounces grape jelly
¾ cup water
1 bottle chili sauce
3 tablespoons lemon juice

1. Combine sauce ingredients and simmer 30 minutes.
2. To make meatballs, tear bread; mix with milk to make paste. Combine with rest of ingredients.
3. Fry one meatball to test for flavor. Correct seasoning if necessary.
4. Shape meatballs with teaspoon. Chill at least one hour.
5. Sauté meatballs. Refrigerate until needed. Add meatballs to sauce. Heat sauce to boiling and simmer for 30 minutes.

Meatballs may be made ahead and frozen. Serve in chafing dish.

Alternate Sauce
1 10-ounce jar of apricot preserves
¼ cup hot barbecue sauce
3 tablespoons lemon juice
½ cup water

Sauerkraut Balls with Delicate Mustard Sauce

1 pound lean, ground round beef
1 16-ounce can sauerkraut
½ cup chopped onion

2 tablespoons flour
2 eggs
*¾ cup mashed potatoes
Italian seasoned bread crumbs

1. Drain sauerkraut; chop a little.
2. Mix meat, well drained sauerkraut, and onion.
3. Add flour, eggs and potatoes; stir together.
4. Roll into 1-inch balls, then roll in crumbs.
5. Deep fry and serve hot with following Delicate Mustard Sauce.

Note: Can be made ahead and frozen. To freeze, place balls on waxed paper lined cookie sheet. When frozen solid, place balls in a plastic bag and return to freezer. Remove as needed and heat in a 350° oven on foil lined pan until heated through.

¾ cup dehydrated potatoes that have been reconstituted according to directions on the package can be substituted for mashed potatoes.

Delicate Mustard Sauce

1 13¾-ounce can chicken broth
½ to 1 teaspoon Dijon mustard, to taste

1 tablespoon lemon juice
3 egg yolks

1. Place chicken broth in top half of double boiler and simmer over direct heat until broth is reduced to about 1 cup.
2. Beat egg yolks. Add lemon juice and ½ cup reduced broth, stirring constantly with a wire whisk to avoid lumps.
3. Place top half of double boiler holding remaining chicken broth over bottom half of double boiler which has ½ inch of boiling water in it.
4. Gradually pour egg yolk mixture into remaining chicken broth, stirring constantly with wire whisk. Continue heating and stirring until thickened (about 5 minutes). Remove from heat.
5. Add mustard to taste.

Note: When ready to serve, reheat sauce in double boiler. Serve sauerkraut balls with toothpicks. Dip in warm sauce to eat.

Steak Tartare I

This is a recipe that makes a hit when served at cocktail parties. It is a slight variation on what is usually done to season ground beef. It was obtained from a gourmet who lost his teeth and ate nothing but steak tartare every night for dinner. No anchovies are included because I don't like them. The recipe calls for Mr. Mustard which is the way it was given to me. It won't work with any other type mustard other than a dijon or dijon style. The two dijon style mustards made in the U.S.A. are Mr. Mustard and Grey Poupon. A true French dijon would be great but by the time it gets to the shelves in this country it has lost its flavor. A pound of this recipe is adequate for an hors d'oeuvre but might only serve two or three as a main course. This recipe for two pounds can be used at a large cocktail party.

2 pounds ground round steak	Ground black pepper
3-4 teaspoons Dijon mustard	Garlic powder (optional)
1 tablespoon chili sauce	Dill weed
1½ tablespoons half and half (or cream)	Parsley flakes
	Paprika
1 small onion, finely grated	Capers
Salt	

1. Place the meat in a mixing bowl and make a large crater in the center. Put in the mustard, chili sauce, half and half, and the grated onion. Sprinkle in some salt, pepper, garlic powder and dill weed to taste. Take a wooden spoon and carefully mix the ingredients into the meat until blended.
2. Place on a serving platter (it can be round or long like a meat loaf.)
3. Garnish the top with parsley flakes, paprika, and capers.

The capers may be placed in a side dish so they can be used optionally. Serve with party rye, melba toast rounds or any other type of bread or cracker.

Steak Tartare II

2 pounds top round, ground three times	½ teaspoon hot sauce
	½ teaspoon freshly ground pepper
1 raw egg	½ bottle chili sauce
Dash A-1 sauce	½ cup chopped sweet onion
1 teaspoon salt	1 can anchovies

1. Mix first seven ingredients together.
2. Place on serving platter and garnish with anchovies.

Note: Serve with party rye and chopped onions in a bowl on the side.

Appetizer Ranch Ribs

2 teaspoons light corn syrup
2 tablespoons corn starch
⅓ cup soy sauce
2 tablespoons Worcestershire
1 teaspoon ginger

¼ cup vinegar
1 clove garlic, crushed
¼ teaspoon salt
½ cup light brown sugar
Dash of Tabasco
4 pounds spareribs

1. Cook first ten ingredients for five minutes.
2. Have butcher crack spareribs into two inch long pieces.
3. Prior to cooking, cut apart and separate into ribs.
4. Simmer in pot of water to cover, add one onion and cook until tender but meat still clings to bone.
5. Drain ribs and chill.
6. When ready to bake place ribs on rack in large pan, and brush with the sauce.
7. Pour sauce over ribs in pan; place in 325° oven. Bake for 1½ hours or until tender and glazed, basting often.

Serving Suggestions: Serve part at a time. Keep remaining hot for platter refills leaving oven turned to 250°. Serve as is or with prepared horseradish to dip in. Can be made as long as two days before and kept in refrigerator.

Cocktail Spareribs

3 pounds spareribs, cracked in 2-3 inch pieces.
1 teaspoon MSG

3 tablespoons soy sauce
½ cup prepared mustard
1 cup brown sugar

1. Bake ribs at 325° for 1½ hours. Drain on paper towels.
2. Make sauce of remaining ingredients.
3. Brush ribs with sauce.
4. Return ribs to 300° oven. Bake 45 minutes, basting several times.

Grilled Flank Steak

½ cup salad oil
¼ cup soy sauce
2 tablespoons vinegar
1 teaspoon powdered ginger

¾ teaspoon garlic salt
3 tablespoons honey
Flank steak
Miniature buns

1. Combine first 6 ingredients.
2. Pour over steak and marinate overnight, turning several times.
3. Remove from marinade.
4. Cook briefly over charcoal (meat should be rare).
5. Slice in thin strips, cutting across grain. Serve on miniature buns as hors d'oeuvre.

For a variation, use the following for marinade, using above procedure.

¼ cup olive oil
¼ cup soy sauce
½ cup red wine
1 clove garlic, crushed

1 onion, thinly sliced
1 teaspoon ginger
Salt and pepper to taste

Grilled Beef Strips

Makes about 20

1 pound round steak, about 1 inch thick
1 clove garlic, thinly sliced
2 tablespoons sherry
1 teaspoon sugar

⅓ cup soy sauce
1-inch piece of fresh ginger, thinly sliced or 1 teaspoon ground ginger

1. Remove fat from meat and slice very thin. (It is easier to do if meat is partially frozen.)
2. Mix remaining ingredients and marinate meat strips in mixture for at least ½ hour.
3. Thread meat on wooden sticks and broil over hot coals on grill or hibachi.

Chicken Fat

Throughout a long and colorful history, Jewish tradition has been known for its steadfast faith, its respect for learning...and its chicken fat, otherwise known as "schmaltz". Melted over heat, with a bit of onion, chicken fat has lent its special deliciousness to everything from mashed potatoes to roast chicken. But its most popular and traditional use is in chopped chicken livers, where its mouth-watering flavor and light cohesiveness give the dish just the right consistency and taste. As an ancient sage once remarked, "Variations may come and go, but chopped liver without chicken fat is like a house without windows."

Chicken Fat Contemporary

1. Wash fat and drain on paper towels.
2. Place in cooking bag with 1 tablespoon chopped onion per pound of chicken fat and 1 tablespoon flour.
3. Twist bag 2 inches from top and fasten with twist tie.
4. Puncture 6 holes in top of bag.
5. Place bag in 2 inch deep baking pan, a little larger than bag.
6. Bake at 275° for 45 minutes.
7. Remove from oven and cool to room temperature.
8. Pull corner of bag over edge of pan and snip with scissors. Then tip pan and pour fat into jar.

Pan should be large enough to contain entire contents of bag in case it should leak.

Rendered Chicken Fat

1 pound raw chicken fat   1 tablespoon salt
2 extra large onions, sliced

1. Cook all ingredients in heavy pot until fat is melted and onion browned.
2. Remove onion and cool. Strain.

Note: Store chicken fat in a jar in refrigerator. Can be kept for a long time. Can be frozen. This recipe is "like Grandma used to make."

Chopped Liver

Get a group of women talking about chopped liver... and for every 5 cooks, you'll have 8 opinions about which is the best recipe. Here are a few versions of "the only way!"

Chopped Chicken Livers

1 pound chicken livers
4 tablespoons rendered chicken fat (p. 94)
1½ cups chopped onions
3 hard-cooked egg yolks
1 teaspoon salt
¼ teaspoon freshly ground black pepper

1. Wash the livers and remove any discolored spots. Drain.
2. Heat 2 tablespoons fat in frying pan; brown the onions in it. Remove the onions.
3. Cook the livers in the fat remaining in the skillet for 10 minutes.
4. Grind or chop the onions, liver and egg yolks until you have a smooth mixture.
5. Add the salt, pepper and remaining fat.
6. Mix and taste for seasoning.

Note: Serve cold with crackers as a spread or on lettuce as an appetizer.

Chicken Liver Pâté I

1 pound chicken livers
8 eggs, hard boiled
1 medium to large size raw onion
Salt and pepper, to taste
2-4 tablespoons chicken fat (p. 94)

1. Boil chicken livers until just done. Drain.
2. When cool, put liver, eggs and onion through grinder.
3. Add salt and pepper to taste and enough chicken fat to hold pâté together.
4. Put in a mold.

Note: Serve with small party rye rounds or crackers. Can be made a day ahead.

Chicken Liver Pâté II

1 pound chicken livers
1 small onion
¾ cup chicken stock
½ teaspoon curry
1 teaspoon salt
½ teaspoon paprika
1 tablespoon Worcestershire
¼ teaspoon pepper
¾ cup butter
Canned consommé (with gelatin)

1. Simmer livers and onion in stock five minutes. Drain.
2. Pour all ingredients into blender, except butter and consommé. Whirl until smooth.
3. Add butter a little at a time.
4. Put into dish and chill.
5. Pour consommé over top. Chill until consommé is jelled.

Make 1 day ahead.

Chicken Liver Mousse

1 pound chicken livers
1½ teaspoons salt
½ teaspoon pepper
2 eggs
2 egg yolks

1 small onion
Few sprigs parsley
2 cups whipping cream
1 cup jellied consommé
1 teaspoon gelatin
¼ cup sherry

1. Place all but last three ingredients in blender, in two installments (half at a time). Blend until smooth; combine.
2. Place in greased bake and serve dish. Place dish in pan of hot water. Bake 50 minutes at 350°. Cool.
3. Soften gelatin in sherry. Add to boiling consommé and stir until dissolved. Chill until partially set.
4. Pour over cooled liver mousse. Decorate with olives.

Suggestions: Serve with crackers to spread. Delicious! Nobody will guess that it takes only a few minutes to prepare.

Mushroom Chicken Liver Pâté

¼ cup butter
½ pound fresh mushrooms, sliced
1 pound chicken livers
1 teaspoon garlic salt
1 teaspoon paprika

⅓ cup finely chopped green onions
½ cup white table wine
3 drops Tabasco
½ cup butter
Salt to taste

1. Sauté the mushrooms, liver, garlic salt, paprika and onion in butter for 5 minutes.
2. Add wine and Tabasco; cover and cook slowly for 5-10 minutes longer.
3. Cool; whirl in blender. Blend in ½ cup of softened butter and salt to taste.
4. Turn into dish; chill overnight.
5. Unmold; garnish with parsley and thin lemon slices.

Mock Pâté de Foie Gras

1 pound chicken livers
1 teaspoon salt
¼ teaspoon nutmeg
⅛ teaspoon ground cloves

1½ teaspoons dry mustard
4 tablespoons minced onions
1 teaspoon anchovy paste
Chicken fat (p. 94)

1. Cook livers in water barely to cover, about 20 minutes. Drain.
2. Put through fine blade of food chopper twice.
3. Add all remaining ingredients except chicken fat and mix well. Blend in sufficient softened chicken fat to bind.
4. Pack in mold and chill for several hours or overnight.

To serve: Unmold on serving tray, decorate with two hard boiled eggs pressed through a sieve. Serve with party rye bread.

Duckling Pâté

Serves 20

1 duck, quartered
3 cups water
2 teaspoons salt
10 peppercorns
1 bay leaf
4 cloves
1 teaspoon Worcestershire

1 12-ounce can chopped black
  olives
½ cup sour cream
¼ teaspoon Tabasco
1 teaspoon salt
1 teaspoon grated onion
12 ounces cream cheese
1 can Sell's liver pâté
¼ cup brandy

1. Stew duck and giblets in water with salt, peppercorns, bay leaf and cloves, until tender. Let cool in broth ½ hour.
2. Pour off broth and let fat rise. Reserve ¾ cup fat.
3. Put meat and giblets through fine grinder of food chopper two times. Discard skin.
4. Add remaining ingredients and ½ cup or less of reserved fat (enough to bind the pâté).
5. Pack into tureen or small serving bowl. Pour remaining ¼ cup fat on top to seal.

A very luxurious pâté. Worth getting greasy fingers. Chill before serving. Can be made a few days ahead. Don't freeze.

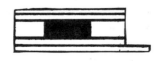

Pâté

1 teaspoon unflavored gelatin
½ can undiluted consommé
1 large can Sell's liver pâté

2 3-ounce packages cream cheese
2 tablespoons lemon juice
Worcestershire
Seasoned salt

1. Soften gelatin in ¼ cup cold consommé. Add to remaining consommé, heated to boiling.
2. Pour thin layer in small mold. Refrigerate until set.
3. Mix pâté, cream cheese and lemon juice. Season to taste with Worcestershire and seasoned salt.
4. Spread into mold, on top of jelled consommé.
5. Pour remaining consommé over pâté.
6. Refrigerate overnight.

Liver Pâté

1 pound liverwurst
⅛ teaspoon dried thyme leaves
1 tablespoon Worcestershire
⅛ teaspoon mace
1 teaspoon ground cloves

1½ tablespoons sherry
1 tablespoon grated onion
¼ teaspoon pepper
¼ cup butter or margarine, softened

1. Peel casing from liverwurst. In medium bowl, mash meat with fork until smooth.
2. Add remaining ingredients, except butter; mix well.
3. Blend in butter until well combined.
4. Pack into serving dish. Cover tightly; refrigerate until ready to use.

Serve with crackers or small slices of rye bread.

Chicken Livers in Brandy

½ cup butter or margarine
3-4 tablespoons brown sugar
1 tablespoon lemon juice

3 tablespoons cognac, brandy or sherry
2 pounds chicken livers

1. Melt shortening. Add brown sugar and lemon juice. Add liquor.
2. Sauté chicken livers in skillet over medium heat until medium done; cover and keep warm at low heat. Do not allow them to dry out; they will get tough.

Note: Serve hot. Skewer on tooth picks. Use nice big chicken livers.

Scrumptious Sausages

Wiener Tidbits

2 large eggs, hard boiled
Grated onion or onion powder, to taste
Salt and pepper, to taste
Mayonnaise
1 pound wieners

1. Peel eggs and chop. Combine with onion, salt, pepper, and enough mayonnaise to hold together.
2. Split each wiener lengthwise almost to the bottom. Fill them with the egg spread. Hold together with 1 or 2 wooden toothpicks.
3. Place on cookie sheet or pan.
4. Heat in 325° oven until heated through, 10-15 minutes.
5. Remove from oven and cut each wiener in 3 or 4 pieces.

Note: Serve warm on toothpicks. Can be made a few days ahead and refrigerated. Place in oven before serving. Wieners can also be filled with cream cheese and served cold.

Drunken Hot Dogs

Serves 6 to 8

1 pound cocktail franks
¾ cup bourbon
1½ cups catsup
½ cup brown sugar
1 tablespoon grated onion (optional)

1. Mix all ingredients together in a saucepan.
2. Simmer over low heat for 1 hour. If it dries out, add a little more bourbon.

Note: Transfer to chafing dish and serve with toothpicks.

Pickled Dog

Ring bologna
2 tablespoons pickling spices
1 red pepper
Distilled vinegar

1. Cut bologna into bite-sized cubes.
2. Pack gently into quart jar.
3. Add pickling spices and red pepper.
4. Fill jar with vinegar. Put lid on jar.
5. Refrigerate for 24 hours before using.

A specialty of Hedrick's General Store, Nashville, Indiana.

This is a great picnic hors d'oeuvre. Serve with toothpicks.

Wieners in Sweet Sauce

1 10-ounce jar currant or apple
   jelly
½ cup dark brown sugar, packed
1 teaspoon dry mustard

1 teaspoon celery seed
⅓ cup cider vinegar
2 pounds wieners or cocktail
   wieners

1. Combine first five ingredients and bring to a boil.
2. Cut wieners into bite size pieces. Heat in sauce.
3. Place heated wieners in sauce in chafing dish.

Note: Any leftover sauce may be frozen and served again.

Cocktail Sausages and Mushrooms

Serves 5 to 6

1 8-ounce can tomato sauce
1 cup dry white wine
¼ teaspoon garlic powder
1 teaspoon oregano

1 teaspoon salt
2 cans drained Vienna sausages
   (cut in half crosswise)
2 cans drained mushroom caps

1. Combine tomato sauce, wine and spices in saucepan. Simmer
   over low heat for five minutes.
2. Add sausages and mushrooms to sauce. Cover and simmer for
   twenty minutes.

Serve in chafing dish.

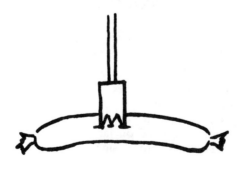

Fishing for Compliments

On a scale of one to ten —
these wonders from the sea rate
high and are sure to hook your
guests.

7

COLD SEAFOODS

Herring Salad

Serves 10

1 16-ounce can red beets, drained
2 16-ounce jars of herring in wine
    sauce, drained (save brine)
1 small can sliced potatoes,
    drained
1 hard cooked egg

1 dill pickle
1 apple
1 cup sour cream
½ cup chopped almonds
1 tablespoon sugar

1. Cut first six ingredients into small cubes.
2. Mix sour cream with brine and onions from herring jar and add sugar and almonds; mix salad well.

Note: An old German recipe. Put in a salad bowl; surround tray with slices of rye bread.

Seviche

Serves 8

1 pound raw scallops
⅓ cup lime juice
½ teaspoon salt

2 teaspoons prepared mustard
½ cup chopped onion
1 hot red pepper, chopped

1. Put raw scallops in collander, pour boiling water over them and drain thoroughly.
2. Place in bowl with lime juice, salt, mustard, chopped onion and red pepper. Let stand at least 3 hours in refrigerator, stirring occasionally.
3. Drain on paper towels.

Serve cold with cocktail sauce. For a milder version, omit onion and pepper.

Artichoke Bottom - Crabmeat

Serves 6

* 1 6-ounce can crabmeat
1-2 teaspoons mayonnaise

6 artichoke bottoms
Capers or parsley

1. Mix drained crabmeat with mayonnaise.
2. Place on top of drained artichoke bottoms.
3. Garnish with capers or parsley.

Elegant and easy.

*See page 26.

Pickled Shrimp Jamaica

Serves 12

1 cup dry white wine
½ cup salad oil
¼ cup garlic vinegar
1 teaspoon seasoned salt

½ teaspoon dried dill weed
4 drops Tabasco
Dash Jamaica allspice
6 cups large cooked, cooled,
   shelled shrimp

1. Mix first seven ingredients.
2. Pour over shrimp.
3. Refrigerate several hours or overnight.

Pickled Shrimp

2½ pounds fresh or frozen shrimp
½ cup celery tops
¼ cup mixed pickling spices
3½ teaspoons salt
2 cups sliced onions
8 bay leaves

Pickling Marinade:
1¼ cups salad oil
¾ cup white vinegar
3 tablespoons capers and juice
2½ teaspoons salt
Dash Tabasco

1. Cover shrimp with boiling water. Add celery, spices and salt.
   Return to boiling point. Remove from heat and let stand,
   covered in boiling water 2 minutes. Then drain, cool with cold
   water.
2. Alternate shrimp and onion in a shallow dish. Add the bay
   leaves.
3. Mix ingredients of pickling marinade. Pour over the shrimp
   and onions. Cover with plastic wrap and chill at least 24
   hours in pickling marinade.

*Note: Transfer shrimp, onion and marinade to serving dish when
ready to serve. Have shrimp forks and small dishes available for
service. Everyone asks for this recipe.
The shrimp in marinade can be kept a week in the refrigerator.
Cover with plastic wrap.*

Marinated Shrimp

3 pounds shrimp
3 cups mayonnaise

Juice from 1½ lemons
1 cup sliced red onion

1. Peel and cook shrimp.
2. Marinate with onion overnight in mixture of mayonnaise and
   lemon juice. Taste should be tart; add more lemon juice, if
   necessary.

Shrimp La Maz

½ cup mayonnaise
½ cup chili sauce
2 tablespoons pickle relish
1 tablespoon chopped pimiento
1 teaspoon chopped green pepper

½ cup chopped celery
1 hard boiled egg, chopped
1 teaspoon prepared mustard
1 teaspoon Worcestershire
2 pounds cooked shrimp

1. Mix all ingredients except shrimp to make sauce. (This may be done 24 hours ahead of time.)
2. Several hours before serving, combine with cooked shrimp.

Serve in large salad bowl with plates and forks.

This recipe is very similar to the delicious appetizer served by the famous Patio La Maz in Palm Beach, Florida. If any of the sauce remains after serving, it makes a very good dressing on a wedge of head lettuce.

HOT SEAFOODS

Crab and Almond Hors d'Oeuvre

¼ cup butter
*1 pound crabmeat
⅔ cup slivered almonds, sautéed

⅓ cup heavy cream
3 tablespoons finely chopped fresh parsley
Salt and pepper

1. Melt butter in chafing dish. Add crabmeat; cook 5 minutes until delicately browned.
2. Add almonds, cream and parsley. Season with salt and pepper to taste. Cook 2 minutes longer.

Serve with toast rounds.

This may also be served in individual shells as a first course. Make ahead and place in shells. Reheat at 300° for 30 minutes or until well warmed.

*See page 26.

Baked Minced Clams

Serves 4-6

3 tablespoons butter or margarine
½ cup chopped onions
2 10-ounce cans minced clams

3 tablespoons mayonnaise
6 tablespoons seasoned bread crumbs
3 tablespoons dried parsley flakes

1. Sauté onions in butter.
2. Add drained minced clams (save half the juice). Mix in remaining ingredients and then add the juice.
3. Bake in 350° oven for 20 minutes.

Serve hot with crackers and a spreader (or with cocktail forks on a plate).

Make in morning and refrigerate until late in afternoon before baking.

Oysters Olympia

Serves 8

2 dozen large fresh oysters
½ cup butter
¼ cup minced chives
1 teaspoon summer savory

⅛ teaspoon pepper
⅛ teaspoon salt
2 teaspoons lemon juice
8 thin slices hot, buttered toast

1. Drain oysters well.
2. Melt butter and sprinkle in chives, savory, pepper, salt and lemon juice. Remove from heat and let stand 5 minutes.
3. Reheat and add oysters. Simmer over low heat until edges of oysters begin to curl.
4. Place oysters on toast and spoon sauce over the top.

Scallops Polonaise

Serves 5 to 6

½ cup dry Madeira
3 tablespoons lemon juice
Whole peel of ½ lemon
½ teaspoon tarragon
½ teaspoon onion salt
2 pounds fresh scallops
1 pound mushrooms, sliced
2 tablespoons butter

½ cup shallots, chopped
1 green pepper, sliced
1 teaspoon dehydrated parsley or 1
  tablespoon fresh parsley,
  chopped
1 small jar sliced pimiento
½ cup sour cream
1 teaspoon caraway seed
Salt and pepper to taste

1. Make marinade by mixing first five ingredients.
2. Place scallops in bowl with marinade; cover tightly. Marinate overnight, stirring once to coat all scallops.
3. Drain scallops, reserving marinade. Heat marinade to boiling. Poach scallops, a few at a time, in simmering marinade for 3 minutes. Drain thoroughly in strainer (they will continue dripping).
4. Reduce remaining marinade over medium heat to 2 tablespoons.
5. Sauté sliced mushrooms, shallots and green pepper in butter. Add parsley.
6. Add poached scallops, pimiento, caraway seed, the reduced marinade and sour cream. Heat just until simmering (do not boil sour cream).
7. Correct seasoning with salt and pepper to taste.
8. If sauce is too thin, thicken with a little Wondra flour.

Note: Serve from chafing dish with plates and fork. This is so good that is will vanish. The same recipe may be used for raw shrimp. (Please note that although this is excellent, it is tricky; be careful.)
1. *Don't boil sour cream.*
2. *The scallops will continue to ooze after draining. The amount of flour needed to thicken will depend on just how "wet" the scallops are.*

Shrimp de Jonghe

Serves 10 to 12

3 pounds boiled shrimp
1 teaspoon salt
1 clove garlic, minced
¾ cup butter
1 cup bread crumbs

⅛ teaspoon pepper
½ teaspoon paprika
Dash of cayenne
½ cup sherry

1. Combine all ingredients except shrimp. Blend well.
2. Place alternate layers of shrimp and crumb mixture in a bake and serve dish, or in 12 individual shells. Last layer should be crumbs.
3. Bake at 400° to heat through.

The baking time will depend on the size of the container and the temperature of food when it is placed in oven. It is important that it be piping hot but not dried out. Individual shells at room temperature may be hot in as little as 8 to 10 minutes. A single container will require around 25 minutes to heat through.

Shrimp Supreme de Jeanne

1 12-ounce package frozen shrimp
1 onion, chopped
⅓ green pepper, diced
2 tablespoons butter
½ cup dry sherry or vermouth

½ cup cream of mushroom soup, undiluted
Salt, pepper, garlic salt, to taste
1 jar sliced pimiento
½ cup grated sharp cheddar
⅓ cup bread crumbs

1. Cook shrimp according to directions on package.
2. Sauté onion and green pepper in butter. Add sherry or vermouth. Simmer until liquid is almost evaporated.
3. Add soup, seasonings, pimiento, and cooked shrimp.
4. Put in casserole. Cover with grated cheddar and bread crumbs.
5. Bake at 325° for 20 to 30 minutes until warmed through.
6. Place under broiler until slightly browned.

Seafood Kabobs

4 to 6 large 12 inch skewers
8 to 12 small 6 inch skewers

1 pound shrimp, cleaned, fresh or frozen (thawed)
1 12-ounce package scallops, fresh or frozen (thawed)
1 jar large stuffed green olives
3 lemons, cut in wedges

Soy Basting Sauce
(makes ¾ cup)
¼ cup soy sauce
¼ cup salad oil
¼ cup lemon juice
¼ cup minced parsley
½ teaspoon salt
Dash of pepper

1. Marinate shrimp and scallops for one hour in Soy Basting Sauce.
2. Alternate scallops, olives, lemon wedges and shrimp on oiled skewers.*
3. Brush generously with Soy Basting Sauce before broiling and frequently while cooking to keep shrimp and scallops moist. Cook 2 to 4 inches from heat 2 to 3 minutes on each side. Broil just long enough to brown scallops as overcooking toughens them.
4. Serve with additional sauce.

Skewer shrimp by pairing—turn the second one upside down and reverse its direction.

Serve on large skewers for outdoor grill or miniature skewers for hibachi. On hibachi skewers, they make "guest do-it-yourself" appetizers. If made on large skewers, they can be served as an entrée with rice.

SEAFOOD MOLDS

Gefilte Fish Mold

Serves 6

* 1 24-ounce jar of gefilte fish in plain broth (6-8 pieces)
2 small packages lemon gelatin
1 cup fish broth

1 4-ounce bottle red horseradish
1 cup boiling water
1 tablespoon lemon juice

1. Drain fish, reserving broth.
2. Mix gelatin and boiling water; stir until dissolved.
3. Add remaining ingredients except fish; pour into greased 1 quart mold; chill.
4. When partially set add whole pieces of fish.

This recipe looks very pretty and tastes very good. Put cherry tomatoes in center of mold.

*See page 115 in *Beginning Again* to make your own gefilte fish.

Crabmeat Mold

Serves 10 to 12

2 small packages lemon gelatin
1½ cups boiling water
1 cup chili sauce
1 cup mayonnaise
2 tablespoons pickle relish
1 cup chopped celery
* 2 7-ounce cans good quality crabmeat

Sauce
2 cups sour cream
2 cups chopped cucumber
1 tablespoon lemon juice
Pinch of sugar
Prepared horseradish

1. Dissolve gelatin in boiling water. Stir in chili sauce and mayonnaise until well blended. Chill until slightly thickened.
2. Stir crabmeat into gelatin with pickle relish and celery.
3. Pour into 6 cup ring mold. Let set overnight until firm.
4. Unmold and serve with cucumber sauce.
5. To prepare sauce: mix unpeeled, chopped, well drained cucumber, sour cream, lemon juice, sugar and enough horseradish to give a slightly sharp taste.

Suggestion: This quickly made crabmeat mold always gets raves. It has a crunchy texture. The sauce makes it especially delicious. It makes an attractive platter with the green sauce in center of pink mold, and little mounds of black olives and cherry tomatoes and sprigs of watercress around mold.
Serve it on a plate with a fork in living room as an only appetizer. A rye curl or cracker is a suggested accompaniment.

*See page 26.

Fish Mold (Tuna or Crabmeat)

1 can tomato soup and ½ can
  water
½ teaspoon dill weed
2 envelopes unflavored gelatin
¼ cup cold water
1 pound cream cheese
¼ cup chopped onion

½ cup chopped celery
2 tablespoons chopped green
  pepper
* 2 6-ounce cans tuna or crabmeat
1 cup mayonnaise
2 dashes Tabasco

1. Bring tomato soup to boil; add dill weed.
2. Soften gelatin in ¼ cup of cold water; add to hot soup.
3. Let soup cool 5 or 10 minutes.
4. Add cream cheese to soup. Stir until dissolved and creamy. Add chopped onion, celery, green pepper and fish. Fold in mayonnaise and Tabasco.
5. Pour into 6 cup mold and chill.

Serve with crackers or small bread to spread. Attractive in a fish shaped mold.

Salmon Mousse

1 envelope unflavored gelatin
½ cup water
2 tablespoons lemon juice
1 medium onion
½ cup sour cream

1 cup mayonnaise
1 cup red salmon
½ teaspoon paprika
1 heaping teaspoon dill weed

1. Soften gelatin in lemon juice. Dissolve in boiling water.
2. Place in blender for half a minute. Add onion, run blender another half minute.
3. Add salmon, mayonnaise, paprika and sour cream; run blender another half minute.
4. Place in greased mold. Chill several hours or overnight.

For a heartier fish flavor, use ½ cup salmon juice instead of water; increase salmon to 1 15-ounce can; increase gelatin to 1½ envelopes or 4 teaspoons.
Serve with cucumber slices. Good!!

Salmon or Shrimp Salad in Gelée

2 tablespoons unflavored gelatin
½ cup cold water
1 pound shrimp or canned salmon,
  chopped
6 hard cooked eggs, chopped
1 cup celery, cut fine
2 tablespoons chopped pimiento

1 cup mayonnaise
1 cup chili sauce
1 tablespoon capers
3 tablespoons lemon juice
½ cup catsup
½ teaspoon sugar
1 tablespoon Worcestershire
¼ teaspoon paprika

1. Soak the gelatin in cold water 5 minutes. Place over hot water until dissolved, mixing lightly and thoroughly.
2. Mix remaining ingredients. Add gelatin.
3. Turn into 6 cup ring mold; chill until firm. Unmold.

*See page 26.

Viva Vegetables

The pick of the garden: a perennial favorite adds the refreshing, crisp and calorie conscious selections to your vignette of vegetables.

8

Antipasto

3 carrots, shredded
½ cup sweet cocktail onions
½ cup green olives, sliced
½ cup pitted ripe olives
1 cup celery, sliced
½ cup dill pickles, chopped
½ cup sweet pickles, chopped
1½ cups raw cauliflower buds

1 small can mushrooms
1 can flat anchovies
1 13-ounce can water packed tuna
    fish
French dressing
Worcestershire
Chili sauce
Mayonnaise

1. Marinate carrots for about an hour in enough French dressing to cover.
2. Add rest of ingredients, well drained. (Use mayonnaise, French dressing, Worcestershire and chili sauce to taste to make the mixture moist.)

No matter what you do it turns out great! Serve with party rye or melba toast.

Antipasto Riviera

½ teaspoon thyme
½ teaspoon rosemary
1 tablespoon whole cloves
1 bay leaf
½ teaspoon oregano
1 cup water
⅓ cup cider vinegar
2¼ cups tomato purée
1 teaspoon salt
½ teaspoons pepper
2 red onions, thinly sliced

1 cauliflower separated into small
    pieces or
    1 eggplant, peeled and cut in
    ½ inch cubes
2 green peppers, thinly sliced
1 13-ounce jar salad olives, sliced
1 6-ounce can pitted black olives,
    sliced

1. To make sauce: put five spices into a cheesecloth bag. Place bag in pot containing water, vinegar, tomato purée, salt and pepper.
2. Bring sauce to a boil and add remaining ingredients. Simmer 25-30 minutes. Chill.

To your surprise, the vegetables will still be crisp. Can be made ahead. Refrigerated, lasts for a week.

Mix and Match Appetizer Salad

3 tablespoons wine vinegar
1½ tablespoons French mustard
⅝ cup olive oil
½ cup mayonnaise
3 inches anchovy paste
1 teaspoon salt
¼ teaspoon pepper
2 tablespoons capers
¾ cup diced celery

1 small cauliflower cut in tiny
  flowerets and cooked 5 minutes
  in boiling salted water
1 14-ounce can tiny artichoke
  hearts or large hearts, cut in
  quarters
2 small potatoes, peeled, boiled,
  diced
½ pound cooked shrimp, cut
  lengthwise in half
1 pound mushroom caps, steamed
  5 minutes in ¼ cup boiling
  salted water and 2 tablespoons
  lemon juice
1 jar Belgian baby carrots

1. Whisk mustard with vinegar. Add oil slowly while stirring.
2. Add salt, pepper, mayonnaise, anchovy paste and whisk until smooth. Add capers and celery.

Just before serving, combine with 4 or more ingredients from second column.

Stuffed Dill Pickle

1. Remove ends of pickle, hollow inside. Invert and drain on paper towels until dry.
2. Fill with any cheese spread.
3. Place in refrigerator to set.
4. Slice into one half inch slices.

A tasty, easy, low calorie snack or an attractive garnish.

Tomato Crab Bites

1 pint cherry tomatoes
¼ cup low calorie mayonnaise-
  type dressing
1 teaspoon lemon juice
¼ teaspoon salt

A few drops bottled hot pepper
  sauce
2 tablespoons chopped green onion
*1 7½-ounce can crabmeat

1. Hollow out the cherry tomatoes. Invert and drain.
2. Blend remaining ingredients.
3. Stuff tomatoes with crab mixture.
4. Refrigerate.

This is a low calorie appetizer, about 16 calories per piece. Can be prepared ahead. Serve on lettuce and chopped ice.

*See page 26.

Caponata

1 large eggplant
Salt
⅔ cup plus 2 tablespoons olive oil
1 medium onion, coarsely chopped
1 15-ounce can tomato sauce
1 clove garlic, minced
½ teaspoon dried oregano
½ teaspoon dried basil

¼ teaspoon pepper
1 cup finely sliced celery
1¼ cups pimiento stuffed olives
2 tablespoons drained capers
1 tablespoon sugar
2 tablespoons red wine vinegar
2 tablespoons minced parsley

1. Cut washed, dried, unpeeled eggplant into 1 inch cubes. Sprinkle lightly with salt.
2. Cook eggplant cubes in ⅔ cup olive oil over moderate heat until brown and almost tender. Drain on paper towels.
3. To same skillet add remaining 2 tablespoons olive oil, onion and garlic. Cook gently, stirring often until onion is golden.
4. Add tomato sauce, basil, oregano, pepper and celery. Cover; simmer 30 minutes.
5. Add eggplant and remaining ingredients and mix well. Cover and simmer until skin on eggplant is tender (approximately 15-30 minutes).
6. Cool; cover tightly and refrigerate.

Serve with crackers or Italian bread. Makes approximately 1½ quarts.

Eggplant Antipasto

Serves 12 plus

⅓ cup olive oil
⅓ cup green pepper
3 cups eggplant, diced (1 large)
1 chopped onion
2 cloves garlic
1 teaspoon salt
1 teaspoon pepper

1 teaspoon oregano
1½ teaspoons sugar
2 tablespoons wine vinegar
¼ cup water
¾ cup mushrooms, sliced
1 10¾-ounce can tomato soup

1. Sauté green pepper, eggplant, onion and garlic in olive oil.
2. Add remaining ingredients. Simmer 45 minutes.

Serve at room temperature on party rye.

It can be made ahead and frozen.

Poor Man's Caviar

Makes 2 cups

1 large eggplant
2 tablespoons oil
1 small onion, finely chopped
1 garlic clove, minced

¼ cup finely chopped green pepper
1½ tablespoons lemon juice
1 teaspoon salt
Coarsely ground pepper to taste

1. Slice eggplant into halves. Oil flat surface, and place them flat side down on a baking pan.
2. Broil three inches from heat for 20-25 minutes or until quite soft.
3. Discard skin and mash pulp well with a fork.
4. Sauté onion, garlic and green pepper in oil.
5. Add lemon juice, salt and pepper.
6. Combine eggplant and onion mixture.
7. Chill two or three hours before serving.

A low cholesterol spread.

Serve with crackers or some kind of chips.

Old Time Eggplant

Serves 6

1 large eggplant
½ cup chopped onion

1 teaspoon oil
Salt and pepper

1. Boil eggplant in covered pot until it is quite soft when pierced with fork.
2. Peel off outer skin.
3. Chop in wooden chopping bowl until fine texture.
4. Add onion and oil. Stir and cool.
5. Add salt and pepper to taste.

This is an old Roumanian recipe contributed by a man whose father used to make it for his family.

It can be prepared 2 days in advance. Serve as a spread with crackers, at room temperature or cold. This can also be used as a cold summer salad or side dish vegetable.

Marinated Vegetables

Marinated Mushrooms

Serves 6 to 8

*1 pound small fresh mushrooms
½ cup olive oil
½ cup red wine vinegar
2 cloves garlic, mashed

2 tablespoons prepared horseradish
½ teaspoon oregano
½ teaspoon salt
Pepper to taste

1. Quickly wash mushrooms.
2. Drop them in boiling water and simmer 5 minutes. Drain.
3. Mix all remaining ingredients in a jar and shake well.
4. Pour marinade over mushrooms, mix well and set aside overnight in the refrigerator before serving.

Can be prepared up to 2 days ahead.

For a quickie version of this recipe use ½ bottle Italian dressing for marinade.

Fresh Mushrooms Marinated

*1 pound fresh mushrooms,
  cleaned and dried
½ cup red wine vinegar
⅔ cup salad oil
2 teaspoons chopped chives
1 teaspoon tarragon

½ clove fresh garlic, minced
½ teaspoon salt
½ teaspoon brown sugar (add
  more if needed)
½ teaspoon peppercorns
1 bay leaf

1. Put all ingredients except mushrooms in a jar, shake well.
2. Add mushrooms. Refrigerate 3 to 4 days.

Marinated Mushrooms or Cauliflower
(Low calorie)

*Mushrooms or cauliflower, cut
  into flowerets

Japanese rice vinegar

1. Clean and dry vegetables.
2. Marinate several hours in Japanese rice vinegar.

The rice vinegar has a mild delicate flavor.

> * *Cut off tough end of mushroom stem.*

Pickled Beans

1 can Blue Lake vertical pack
  whole green beans
1 tablespoon tarragon vinegar

Wine vinegar
1 teaspoon salad herbs

1. Drain half of juice from can of beans.
2. Add tarragon vinegar and herbs and fill can with wine vinegar.
3. Let stand overnight in refrigerator. Drain and rinse off herbs before serving.

92 calories per whole recipe. Also good with beets, mushrooms or artichokes.

Fagioli Leonardo
Marinated Beans

1 7-ounce package Minestrone
  beans or
  2 ounces chick peas
  2 ounces lentils
  2 ounces kidney beans
  2 ounces small white beans

¾ cup Italian salad dressing
3 tablespoons minced onions
½ teaspoon oregano
½ teaspoon basil
3 tablespoons sliced pimiento

1. Cover beans with water. Soak for 3 hours. Drain.
2. Cover beans with fresh water; bring to boil and simmer 1½ hours or until beans are tender. Drain.
3. Place in covered jar with remaining ingredients.
4. Marinate overnight. Drain before serving.

This delicious vegetable keeps at least a week in refrigerator. It is an interesting addition to an antipasto tray or it can be served as an hors d'oeuvre with plate and fork. This bean mixture makes a good salad or side dish accompaniment.

Quick Cucumbers

6 cucumbers
2 onions
¼ cup sugar
1 cup vinegar

1 teaspoon dill seed
1 teaspoon mustard seed
1 teaspoon celery seed
1 tablespoon salt
½ teaspoon cream of tartar

1. Peel and slice cucumbers and onions.
2. Boil remaining ingredients together for 1 minute and pour over vegetables.
3. Marinate in refrigerator overnight.

117

Brussel Sprouts Vinaigrette

1 20-ounce package frozen brussel
   sprouts
3 tablespoons minced pimiento
2 tablespoons minced green pepper
2 tablespoons minced green onion
½ teaspoon salt
Dash of pepper
1 cup Italian salad dressing
Grated Parmesan cheese

1. Follow directions for cooking on package of frozen brussel sprouts. (Do not overcook.)
2. Drain and cool. Combine the sprouts with all the other ingredients. Toss gently.
3. Cover and chill overnight or 1 to 2 days before serving.
4. Drain. Serve topped generously with grated Parmesan cheese.

Marinated Vegetables

* 2 cups mushrooms, cut up
1 cup cut green beans, cooked
1 pint box cherry tomatoes
1 cucumber, sliced
½ cup Italian dressing

Combine vegetables with Italian dressing and marinate for a few hours.

Marinated Pimientos

3 tablespoons red wine vinegar
2 cloves garlic, minced
1 bay leaf
½ teaspoon salt
½ teaspoon pepper
2 tablespoons olive oil
2 tablespoons chili sauce
2 7-ounce jars pimientos
Anchovies
Ripe olives
Lemon juice

1. Simmer first 5 ingredients in saucepan 5 minutes.
2. Blend in olive oil and chili sauce. Pour over pimientos.
3. Marinate 3 hours
4. Drain pimientos. Garnish with anchovies and ripe olives.
5. Drizzle lemon juice over all.

Serve alone or as part of an antipasto tray.

Asparagus Hors d'Oeuvres

1 bunch fresh asparagus, washed
   and tough ends cut off
1 hibachi stick for every asparagus
   stalk
1 cup Green Goddess dressing
1 cup Italian dressing

1. Push the stick into the end of the asparagus.
2. Mix together Green Goddess and Italian dressings.
3. Pour mixture over asparagus and marinate overnight.

*See page 116.

Pickled Carrots

1 16-ounce jar whole carrots
¼ cup chopped onions
½ cup low calorie Italian dressing

¼ teaspoon salt
½ teaspoon dill weed
1 tablespoon parsley
Dash of pepper

1. Combine dressing with rest of ingredients.
2. Cover and refrigerate overnight.

This recipe can be left in refrigerator for several weeks.

Serve alone or as part of an antipasto tray.

Marinated Carrots

5 cups carrots (sliced or julienne)
   cooked, drained and cooled
1 medium onion
1 medium green pepper
1 10¾-ounce can cream of tomato
   soup
½ cup salad oil

¾ cup vinegar
1 teaspoon prepared mustard
1 teaspoon Worcestershire
1 cup sugar
1 teaspoon salt
½ teaspoon pepper

1. Cut onion and green pepper in rounds and arrange over carrots.
2. Mix remaining ingredients and pour over vegetables. Cover tightly.
3. Marinate in refrigerator 24 hours.

Stuffed Radishes

Radishes
Chive cream cheese

Caviar

1. Clean radishes. Place in water in refrigerator for one hour to crisp.
2. Hollow out center of radish. Cut stem end off flat so radish will stand.
3. Fill hollow half full with chive cream cheese. Fill up with caviar.

Red Radishes

Radishes
Salt

Cream cheese, bleu cheese or
   cheddar

1. Carefully scoop out radishes with vegetable peeler, leaving firm shell.
2. Sprinkle with salt, and stuff with softened cheese.

Celery or Endive Stalks

General Directions

1. Wash celery or endive and drain on paper towels.
2. Fill with desired stuffing.
3. Cut into 1 to 3 inch lengths.
4. Garnish with paprika, if desired.

Fillings For Celery or Endive Stalks

Sardine Stuffing

1 can boneless, skinless oil packed
    sardines
2 tablespoons mayonnaise

1 tablespoon pickle relish
2 teaspoons lemon juice
Salt and pepper to taste

1. Drain and mash sardines.
2. Add remaining ingredients and mix well.
3. Stuff celery with sardine filling. Sprinkle with paprika.

Peanut Stuffing

2 3-ounce packages cream cheese,
    softened
¼ cup peanut butter
2 tablespoons cream

1 tablespoon finely chopped onion
½ teaspoon curry powder
½ cup chopped salted peanuts

1. In small bowl, cream the cheese and peanut butter together, using a wooden spoon.
2. Blend in cream, onion and curry powder.
3. Fill stalks with mixture and sprinkle with chopped peanuts.
4. Refrigerate at least 30 minutes before serving.

Brazil Nut Stuffing

2 3-ounce packages cream cheese
1 tablespoon grated onion
¼ teaspoon salt

Dash of Tabasco
½ cup chopped Brazil nuts

1. Soften cream cheese to room temperature.
2. With a wooden spoon, beat cheese with onion, salt and Tabasco until fluffy.
3. Stir in ¼ cup nuts.
4. Fill stalks with cheese mixture. Sprinkle with remaining nuts.
5. Refrigerate at least 30 minutes before serving.

Spicy Bleu Cheese Stuffed Celery

1½ ounces cream cheese
1 tablespoon Worcestershire

¼ cup bleu cheese
Chopped parsley

1. Mix cheeses and Worcestershire.
2. Cut washed celery stalks in serving pieces and stuff with mixture.
3. Sprinkle with parsley and chill until serving time.

Shrimp Stuffed Celery

1 8-ounce package cream cheese
Salt and pepper to taste
1 teaspoon Worcestershire

1½ teaspoons lemon juice
1½ cups chopped shrimp
3 tablespoons chopped black olives

1. Blend cream cheese with seasonings until smooth.
2. Add chopped shrimp and olives.
3. Stuff celery stalks. Sprinkle with paprika.

Pistachio Stuffing

1 3-ounce package cream cheese,
   softened
½ teaspoon Worcestershire

½ teaspoon lemon juice
1 tablespoon finely chopped
   pistachio nuts

1. Blend cream cheese, Worcestershire and lemon juice in a small bowl, until smooth. Stir in pistachio nuts.
2. Fill stalks, and garnish with additional slivered pistachio nuts.

Celery Stuffed with Roquefort Cheese

½ cup Roquefort cheese
½ cup soft butter or margarine

¼ cup finely chopped watercress

1. Cream together cheese and butter and blend in watercress.
2. Fill centers of celery stalks and chill before serving.

Stuffed Celery Tartare

1. See page 91 for Steak Tartare recipes.
2. Fill celery stalks with meat; garnish with capers.

Artichoke Hors d'Oeuvres

General directions for preparing artichokes.

1. Remove any discolored leaves and the small leaves at the base of the artichoke.
2. Slice 1 inch off the top and discard.
3. Snip off points of the leaves with kitchen shears.
4. Trim stem flat and even with the artichoke base so it can sit level.
5. Rinse artichoke under cool water to clean.
6. (For 4 artichokes) Bring 6 quarts of water to boil in a large kettle. Add 2 tablespoons lemon juice to the water to prevent the vegetable from discoloring. For a different taste also add 2 tablespoons tarragon vinegar.
7. Add artichokes to boiling water and steam for 30 to 40 minutes until artichoke is tender.
8. Remove artichokes from water carefully (use tongs or two large spoons) and place upside down to drain.
9. Chill artichokes for at least 4 hours before serving.
10. To eat artichokes, pluck leaves one at a time. Dip base of leaf into sauce. Turn leaf meaty side down and draw between teeth scraping off meaty portion. Discard leaf.
11. When all outer leaves have been removed, a center cone of small light-colored leaves covering the fuzzy center choke will be exposed. Pull or cut off cone of leaves. Slice off fuzzy choke with grapefruit knife and discard, leaving the best part, the artichoke heart. This can be cut into bite-sized pieces and dipped in the sauce.
12. The choke may be removed before serving if desired. Open each artichoke like a flower to reach the inside and pull out the tender center cone of leaves, scrape off exposed choke with spoon. This is especially nice if serving as a first course at a dinner. The center cavity may be filled with sauce or dip.

Suggestion: Any dips or sauces can be served with the artichokes — lemon or garlic butter, hollandaise sauce, or mock hollandaise, Thousand Island dressing, your favorite dip. See chapters on sauces and dips.

Quiches

An assortment of creamy, marvelous quiches that do a double take: either as an hors d'oeuvre or as a hearty main dish. A bite or a slice, they'll have the crust to ask for more.

9

General Instructions for Quiches

1. Frozen pie crusts can be used to save the time of preparing your own pastry.
2. To prevent crust from becoming soggy, bake at 400° for 5 minutes before filling.
3. IMPORTANT: Place cooked quiche on a wire rack to cool for 10 minutes before cutting.
4. To prepare quiche in advance: Prepare crust and bake for 5 minutes at 400°. Mix filling ingredients. Refrigerate both. When ready to bake, stir filling to blend, pour into shell and bake as directed in recipe.
5. For miniature quiches: Fit pastry inside small souffle dishes or individual tart pans. Bake 4 minutes at 400° or until very lightly browned. Cool. Fill with desired filling. Bake at 350° for 30 minutes or until set.
6. For a lower calorie quiche, substitute skim milk for half and half or cream in any quiche recipe.

Pastry for Quiche Crust

2 9-inch crusts

2 cups sifted flour
½ teaspoon salt
⅔ cup butter

3 tablespoons vegetable shortening
¼ cup milk

1. Stir salt into flour.
2. Cut shortenings into dry ingredients until crumbly and size of peas.
3. Sprinkle milk over flour and shortening mixture, stirring lightly with fork to blend. DON'T OVER-MIX.
4. Shape into 2 balls with hands. Chill 1 hour.
5. Roll out, using as little flour as possible. (Use pastry cloth and rolling pin cover to prevent sticking.)
6. Place crust in pan, pressing firmly around edge. Do not stretch crust, but rather ease it in so that the crust doesn't shrink away from side of pan while baking.
7. Bake at 400° for 5 minutes. Cool on wire rack. Fill and bake as directed in quiche recipe.

Shrimp Quiche

1 9-inch pie crust
3 tablespoons grated Parmesan
  cheese
½ cup chopped cooked shrimp
½ cup grated Swiss cheese

3 egg yolks
¾ cup light cream
Dash Tabasco
½ teaspoon salt

1. Bake pie crust at 400° for 5 minutes and cool.
2. Place the Parmesan cheese, chopped shrimp and Swiss cheese in the pie shell.
3. Mix the egg yolks, cream, Tabasco and salt and fill shell with the mixture.
4. Bake in a 350° oven for 45 minutes.
5. Cool 10 minutes before cutting.

Nova Scotia Quiche

1 partially baked 9-inch pie shell
4 eggs
2 egg yolks
2 cups heavy cream
2 tablespoons tomato paste
⅛ teaspoon white pepper

⅛ teaspoon nutmeg, or a few
  grinds fresh
¼ teaspoon paprika
¼ pound Gruyère cheese, grated
*½ pound Nova Scotia salmon
  (lox)

1. Bake pie crust at 400° for 5 minutes and cool.
2. Beat eggs and egg yolks in a bowl until blended.
3. Add cream and tomato paste; season with pepper, nutmeg, paprika.
4. Chop Nova Scotia salmon and add to egg-cream mixture.
5. Sprinkle cheese on bottom of pie shell and pour in salmon-cream mixture. Bake 25 to 30 minutes at 400°.
6. Cool 10 minutes before cutting.

*See page 114 of BEGINNING AGAIN to make your own lox.

Crabmeat Quiche

½ cup mayonnaise
2 tablespoons flour
2 beaten eggs
½ cup milk
*1 6-ounce can crabmeat, drained
  and flaked

8 ounces natural Swiss cheese,
  grated
⅓ cup sliced green onions
2 tablespoons butter
1 9-inch pie shell

1. Bake pie crust at 400° for 5 minutes and cool.
2. Combine mayonnaise, flour, eggs and milk; mix until blended.
3. Sauté onions in butter.
4. Add crabmeat, cheese and sautéed onions to above mixture.
5. Pour into pastry-lined plate.
6. Bake at 350° for 40 to 45 minutes.

*See page 26.

Tomato Quiche

1 10-ounce package piecrust mix (or make your own 13-inch pie crust)

2 ripe tomatoes or 1 14-ounce can salad style tomatoes, drained

1 egg white, slightly beaten

3 eggs

2 tablespoons butter or margarine, melted

1½ teaspoons salt

3 cups heavy cream

½ cup + 1 tablespoon grated Gruyère or Swiss cheese

1. Prepare piecrust mix as label directs. Use only ¾ of the pastry. Save the rest for something else.
2. On a lightly floured surface or between two sheets of waxed paper, roll out a 13-inch circle. Line sides and bottom of a 9-inch spring form or soufflé dish. Pastry should come up about 2 inches on sides.
3. Bake pie crust at 400° for 5 minutes and cool.
4. Scald tomatoes if you are using fresh ones and peel skin off and remove seeds. Chop coarsely. Drain on paper towels.
5. Brush bottom of pastry shell very lightly with some slightly beaten egg white.
6. In medium bowl, combine the eggs, cream, butter and salt. Beat until thoroughly combined — do not beat too hard. Stir in ½ cup grated cheese.
7. Put tomatoes in pie shell. Pour cheese filling into shell and sprinkle top with 1 tablespoon cheese.
8. Bake 55 minutes in 375° oven, until golden brown.
9. Cool 5 to 10 minutes and then loosen edge of pastry from side of pan. Remove side from springform. Place bottom of pan on serving plate and serve warm.

If baked in soufflé dish it is not necessary to remove quiche.

Swiss Spinach Quiche

*1 8-ounce can refrigerator
  crescent rolls
1 8-ounce package natural Swiss
  cheese slices, cut into thin strips
½ cup grated Parmesan cheese
3 tablespoons flour
1¾ cups milk

4 eggs, beaten slightly
¼ teaspoon salt
⅛ teaspoon pepper
⅛ teaspoon nutmeg
1 10-ounce package frozen chopped spinach

1. Separate crescent dough into large rectangles; place in bottom of greased 13 x 9 casserole in single layer. Press and seal holes. Cover bottom of casserole and ¼ inch up the sides.
2. In mixing bowl, toss cheeses with flour.
3. Combine milk, eggs and seasonings. Mix with cheeses.
4. Add thoroughly drained spinach (press out moisture).
5. Pour into crescent dough crust; bake 50 minutes at 350°.

Note: Cut into small squares. Serve warm. Can be frozen already baked and then reheated.

*A pastry crust may be substituted.

Quiche Lorraine

*Serves 6 as main dish
10-12 for appetizer*

Pastry for a deep dish 9-inch pie
  plate or a 10-inch quiche dish
½ pound bacon
½ pound Swiss or Gruyère cheese,
  shredded
4 eggs, beaten
1 tablespoon flour

½ teaspoon salt
½ teaspoon celery salt
¼ teaspoon cayenne
¼ teaspoon nutmeg
1½ cups light cream
1 cup chopped onion
2 tablespoons butter

1. Bake pastry at 400° for 5 minutes. Cool.
2. Fry bacon until crisp; drain and crumble. Reserve 2 tablespoons bacon for trim.
3. Place remaining bacon in pie shell and add cheese.
4. Sauté onion in butter.
5. Combine remaining ingredients with onion and pour over cheese.
6. Sprinkle reserved bacon over the top.
7. Bake at 350° for 30 to 40 minutes before serving.

¾ cup sliced ham may be substituted for the bacon.

For vegetarian quiche, omit bacon.

Cheese and Onion Quiche

Serves 6 to 8

1 9-inch pie shell
1 cup onions, thinly sliced
2 tablespoons butter or margarine
½ pound natural Swiss cheese, grated
1 tablespoon flour

3 eggs
1 cup milk
½ teaspoon salt
⅛ teaspoon pepper or seasoned pepper

1. Pre-bake pie shell partially about 5 minutes at 400°. Cool.
2. In small skillet sauté onions in butter until tender; turn into pastry shell.
3. Toss grated cheese with flour; sprinkle over onions.
4. Beat eggs well, add milk, salt and pepper. Pour over cheese.
5. Bake at 350° for 45 minutes, until knife inserted in middle of pie comes out clean.
6. Let stand 10 minutes. Cut in small wedges.

Quick Onion Soup Quiche

8 to 10 appetizer servings

Pastry for a 9-inch pie shell
3 slices Provolone cheese
3 tablespoons dehydrated onion soup mix
½ cup grated Swiss cheese
3 eggs

1 egg yolk
2 cups half and half
¼ teaspoon salt
¼ teaspoon pepper
1 tablespoon butter or margarine

1. Line 9-inch pie pan with pastry.
2. Bake pastry at 400° for 5 minutes. Remove from oven and cool before filling.
3. Place slices of Provolone cheese on bottom of pie shell.
4. Combine onion soup mix and Swiss cheese and sprinkle over Provolone cheese.
5. Lightly beat eggs, egg yolk, cream, salt and pepper; pour into shell.
6. Brown butter and pour over top.
7. Bake at 375° about 30 to 35 minutes or until knife inserted into center comes out clean.
8. Remove from oven and let stand 10 minutes before cutting.

Sauces

The topper adds spice to the life of many dishes. Ladle these on and feel the glow of compliments to the chef.

Seafood Cocktail Sauce

1 bottle chili sauce
1 tablespoon horseradish
2 tablespoons sweet pickle relish
4 dashes Worcestershire
6 dashes Tabasco
6 diced stuffed olives (medium size)

2 tablespoons capers
1 large lemon, juiced
Good dashes of parsley flakes, dill weed, celery salt, paprika, lemon pepper, salt and medium ground black pepper

1. Mix all ingredients with spoon, seasoning to taste.
2. Store in covered container in refrigerator.

Suggestion: Good with crab, lobster, oyster or any seafood combination. Keeps quite a while. Does a good job of opening up your sinuses.

Sauce Louis

Makes 1½ cups

1 cup mayonnaise
¼ cup chili sauce
1 teaspoon Worcestershire
2 tablespoons lemon juice

1 tablespoon dehydrated onion
¼ cup chopped green pepper
2 tablespoons chopped capers

Combine and serve with shrimp, crab or lobster.

Remoulade Sauce

Makes 2 cups

1 cup mayonnaise
1 tablespoon pickle relish
1 tablespoon chopped capers
1 teaspoon chopped parsley or
  ½ teaspoon dehydrated
¼ teaspoon chopped tarragon
1 teaspoon anchovy paste

1 tablespoon Dijon mustard
1 teaspoon finely chopped onion
2 chopped hard-boiled eggs
2 tablespoons chopped celery
1 teaspoon horseradish
Dash of cayenne

Mix and let stand several hours before serving to allow flavors to blend.

Note: This makes sufficient sauce to mix with 3 pounds cooked shrimp or crab.

Mock Hollandaise Sauce

Makes about ½ cup

¼ cup sour cream
2 tablespoons lemon juice
3 egg yolks

½ teaspoon salt
1 tablespoon water

1. Mix well and put over boiling water in small double boiler.
2. Stir until thickened.

Blender Mayonnaise

Makes 1¼ cups

1 egg
1 teaspoon tarragon vinegar
1 teaspoon red wine vinegar

1 tablespoon lemon juice
1 teaspoon salt
Few grinds fresh pepper
1 cup salad oil

1. Beat all ingredients except oil in blender 1 minute.
2. Add oil a little at a time.
3. Beat at high speed until thick.

*Mock Sour Cream

¾ cup smooth cottage cheese
3 tablespoons buttermilk
2 tablespoons lemon juice

Few grains pepper
1½ teaspoons salt

Combine above ingredients, adding more salt, pepper and lemon juice to taste.

A good low calorie, low cholesterol substitute for sour cream. Dill weed, basil or tarragon may be added for variety.

---

*Mock Sour Cream can be satisfactorily substituted for sour cream to adapt many dip recipes for Low Cholesterol diets.

Hollandaise Sauce
Food processor method

6 large egg yolks
4 tablespoons lemon juice
½ teaspoon salt

Few grinds pepper
Pinch cayenne
1 cup sweet butter

1. Place first 5 ingredients in food processor fitted with steel knife.
2. Turn machine on and off immediately.
3. Heat butter almost to boiling point.
4. Turn machine on and add melted butter in a slow steady stream. Process until all of butter is added.
5. Pour into a serving bowl. Cover with plastic wrap. Place in a pan of warm water until ready to use.

If sauce curdles, whisk in 1-2 tablespoons of hot water.

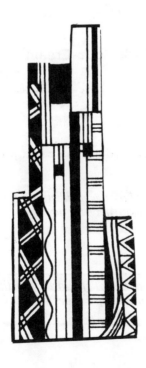

Tureen Cuisine

A "souper" starter for any feast. Some like them hot. Some like them cold. Whatever your taste, they'll bowl you over.

11

SOUP SERVICE

The Butler did it—in the elegant past. But this is the era of "do-it-yourself"...so serve your soup with casual chic from mugs and a pretty ceramic tureen in your living room. Or dig out those wedding present punch bowl sets—perfect for cold soups.

Tip: For that extra touch that shows you care, serve cold soups in chilled mugs and hot soups in warmed mugs.

Whenever recipe calls for canned soup, this refers to a 10¾-ounce can unless otherwise specified.

Hot Soups

Matzo Balls

*3 tablespoons chicken fat at room temperature
2 large eggs
½ teaspoon dehydrated parsley or 1½ teaspoons fresh parsley
1 teaspoon salt
**⅓ cup matzo meal or matzo cake meal

1. Beat chicken fat, eggs, parsley and salt with fork.
2. Stir in matzo meal.
3. Chill in refrigerator for 1 hour or more.
4. Roll into 1½ inch balls.
5. Drop into 2 quarts boiling water.
6. Cover pot and boil slowly for 30 minutes.
7. Transfer matzo ball with slotted spoon to pot of chicken soup.

May be prepared in advance and frozen. Thaw before rewarming. Makes 8-10 matzo balls.

*See page 94.

**Matzo cake meal makes a lighter and fluffier product.*

World's Greatest Vegetable Soup

Serves 16

12 cups water
2 16-ounce cans V-8 juice
4 large carrots (cut in 1 inch slices)
1 3-inch diameter onion (chopped coarse)
1 chunk raw cabbage (size of a man's fist) chopped very coarse
2 10-inch celery stalks, plus leaves, chopped coarse

1 teaspoon salt
1 package Knorr's vegetable soup mix
1 package dry onion soup mix
½ medium green pepper (chopped fine)
1 teaspoon dried parsley
2 beef bouillon cubes
4 ounces uncooked extra-fine cut noodles

1. In large covered pot, bring water and V-8 to a boil. Add carrots, green pepper, onion, cabbage, celery and reduce heat to simmer. Stir frequently with wooden spoon.
2. After 2 hours add all the rest of the ingredients except the noodles and simmer for 30 minutes.
3. Add noodles and cook 10 more minutes.

Holler "soup's on" and stand back so you won't get trampled.

This will make a gallon of soup. Plenty to eat and some for your relatives and freezer. As long as you're going to all this damn trouble you may as well make enough to be worthwhile, I always say.

P.S. You will have a lot of raw vegetables left over, so, in a large bowl, finely chop up the rest of the cabbage, and green pepper, 2 stalks celery, one carrot, one small onion, ¼ teaspoon celery seed, ⅛ teaspoon dill weed, 4 shakes seasoned salt. Then pour one 8 ounce bottle of Marzetti's slaw dressing over it all. Mix well and you've got the **WORLD'S GREATEST COLESLAW.**

Lentil Soup

1 package dried lentils
6 cups water
Ham bone or ¾ pound beef short
 ribs
1 onion, chopped

½ cup diced celery
½ cup sliced carrots
1 teaspoon sugar
1 teaspoon salt
¼ teaspoon thyme
Hot dogs

1. Soak lentils in water to cover, overnight.
2. Next day, drain lentils. Add 6 cups water. Add all other ingredients.
3. Simmer, covered, about 1½ hours.
4. Before serving, thin to desired thickness with milk. Add hot dog, sliced.

It can be made ahead and frozen.

Marrowfat Bean Soup

1 package marrowfat beans
8 stalks celery, chopped
5 carrots, chopped
1 large or 2 small onions

1 tomato
¼ to 1 teaspoon salt
Pepper
A few shakes of paprika, optional
Large ham bone with meat clinging
 to it

1. Soak marrowfat beans overnight.
2. Pour off water.
3. In large pan or 3 quart Dutch oven, boil beans in fresh water to cover. Jackets on beans will loosen.
4. Pour off hot water.
5. Adding fresh water to cover, bring to boil beans, celery, carrots, onions, tomato and seasoning.
6. Add ham bone.
7. Lower heat and simmer 3 to 4 hours. Season to taste.

Full bodied and thick.

Can be served in mugs before dinner or can be a meal in itself.

Cincinnati Chili

2 pounds ground beef
1 quart water
2 medium sized onions, grated
2 8-ounce cans tomato sauce
5 whole allspice
½ teaspoon red pepper
1 teaspoon ground cumin seed
4 tablespoons chili powder

½ ounce bitter chocolate
4 cloves garlic, minced
2 tablespoons vinegar
1 large bay leaf
5 whole cloves
2 teaspoons Worcestershire
1½ teaspoons salt
1 teaspoon cinnamon

1. Add ground beef to water in 4 quart pot, stir until beef separates to a fine texture. Boil slowly for half an hour.
2. Add all other ingredients. Stir to blend, bringing to a boil; reduce heat and simmer uncovered for about 3 hours. Last hour, pot may be covered after desired consistency is reached.
3. Remove bay leaf.
4. Chili should be refrigerated overnight so that fat can be lifted from top before reheating.

Cincinnati Chili has enjoyed national fame since the much publicized Congressional Chili debate.

Serve it in one of the following traditional styles:

Chili Plain
Chili and Spaghetti
3 way - chili, spaghetti, and shredded cheddar cheese
4 way - chili, spaghetti, cheddar and onion
5 way - chili, spaghetti, cheddar, onion and beans
Coney Island - a frankfurter in a bun topped with chili, cheese and onions or any of the above ingredients

There is nothing in any of these combinations that an antacid can't remedy!

Beef Barley Soup

Serves 8

2½ quarts water
1 soup bone with marrow
2 pounds chuck
3 scallions, minced
3 packets G. Washington's rich
   brown seasonings

1 teaspoon salt
Dash of pepper
3 ribs celery, diced
½ cup barley

1. Bring water to a boil. Add all ingredients except barley.
   Reduce heat to simmer and let cook about three hours.
2. Remove meat and bone. When meat is cool, cut into small
   pieces and return to soup. Add barley; let simmer one hour or
   more.
3. Chill overnight. Remove congealed fat.
4. Heat and serve.

Best when made ahead. May be frozen.

Oxtail soup

Serves 8

1 pound lean stew beef
1 pound oxtails
8 ounces cooking sherry
2 cans consomme
2 cans beef bouillon
1 teaspoon Worcestershire
3 bay leaves
1 teaspoon seasoned salt

½ teaspoon MSG
1 teaspoon Beaumonde seasoning
1 bouillon cube
1 large can stewed tomatoes
4 carrots
1 large onion
3 or 4 stalks celery
1 tablespoon chopped parsley
Water

1. Put all ingredients in large size pressure cooker. Fill with
   water to within 1½ inches of top of cooker.
2. When cooker is at height of pressure, let cook for 45 minutes.
   Let cooker cool completely before taking off lid.
3. Remove meat and oxtails; cut meat from bones. Purée soup
   and meat in food processor or blender.
4. Let soup cool completely, taking off fat.
5. Reheat before serving.

Freezes well. Serve in heated mugs.

Elegant King Crab Chowder

*1 7½-ounce can Alaska king crab
1 can condensed potato soup
1 can condensed tomato soup
1 can condensed beef consommé
1 soup can water

1 cup light cream
¾ cup diced celery
1 tablespoon freeze-dried chives
Salt and pepper
3 tablespoons sherry wine
(optional)

1. Break crab into bite sized pieces.
2. Combine soups and water in a saucepan and heat to boiling.
3. Add light cream, crab, celery and chives. Season to taste with salt and pepper.
4. Heat again just to boiling. Add sherry and serve in warm bowls.

Can be made ahead—add sherry when ready to serve.

Palo Alto Shrimp Bisque

Serves 4

3 slices stale bread
2 tablespoons bacon grease or margarine
1 tablespoon chopped onion
1 tablespoon parsley

Salt and pepper to taste
1 crumbled bay leaf
2 cans condensed tomato soup
1 4-ounce can tiny shrimp

1. Soak bread in enough water to soften. Put into fry pan with grease, onion and all seasonings and cook briefly (as for chicken stuffing).
2. Add soup and equal quantity of water.
3. Heat, stir.When hot and ready to serve, add drained shrimp.

This simple version of a homemade soup has its origins in New Orleans.

*See page 26.

Manhattan Clam Chowder

Serves 6

3 slices bacon, finely diced
4 cups boiling water
1½ teaspoons salt
2 cups diced potatoes
1 cup finely diced carrots
1 cup finely diced celery
1 cup chopped onion

10 cooked fresh or 1 10-ounce can
   clams, finely chopped
¾ cup strained clam juice
1 cup stewed canned tomatoes
½ teaspoon thyme
¼ teaspoon pepper
3 tablespoons butter or margarine
3 tablespoons enriched flour

1. Dice bacon and cook slightly.
2. Add boiling water, salt, potatoes, carrots, celery and onion; simmer uncovered 15 minutes or until vegetables are *nearly* tender.
3. Add clams and juice, chopped tomatoes, thyme and pepper.
4. Melt butter; blend in flour and carefully stir into chowder.
5. Simmer 15 minutes longer.

New England Clam Chowder

Serves 4

1 package Knorr Cream of Leek
   Soup
2 cups milk

1 cup water or 1 cup juice from
   clams
1 or 2 cans minced clams, drained

1. Combine soup mix and milk. Bring to boil. Cover and simmer, stirring occasionally over low heat for 10 minutes.
2. Remove lid. Add water or clam juice and drained clams.

Serve piping hot in mugs.

Quick Clam Chowder

1 11-ounce can clam chowder
1 10-ounce can minced clams
Half and half

1 8-ounce can sliced mushrooms
Salt and pepper

1. Pour mushroom juice and clam juice in empty chowder can. Add half and half to fill can.
2. Mix with clam chowder. Add mushrooms, salt and pepper to taste. Heat just to boiling point.

Serve imediately in heated mugs.

Zucchini Soup

Serves 8

2 onions, chopped
¼ cup butter
8 cups sliced zucchini or cucumbers
4 cups chicken broth

2 teaspoons tarragon vinegar
2 teaspoons dill weed
2 tablespoons cream of wheat or 2 boiled potatoes
Parmesan cheese or sour cream

1. In Dutch oven sauté onions in butter until wilted. Add sliced zucchini or cucumber, chicken broth, vinegar, dill, salt and pepper to taste.
2. Bring to a boil. Add cream of wheat or boiled potatoes. Simmer 25 minutes.
3. Mix in blender until smooth.

A Vermont recipe. Can be made ahead and frozen. Serve hot topped with Parmesan, or serve cold topped with sour cream.

Onion Soup

Serves 6

5 cups thinly sliced onions
¼ pound margarine
2 cans consommé
2 cans water
1 cup sherry

2 tablespoons flour (Wondra)
1 tablespoon sugar
1 clove garlic, minced
Chopped parsley
Salt to taste
¼ teaspoon thyme

1. Brown onions lightly in the margarine. Pour off excess margarine.
2. Add the other ingredients and simmer very slowly for 2 hours, covered.

Make a day ahead. Remove hardened fat before warming.

When ready to serve, heat soup to boiling, pour into bake and serve casserole. Cover with 6 slices of toasted French bread. Sprinkle with ¼ cup Parmesan and ¾ cup grated Gruyère cheese. Heat in 275° oven until cheese melts — about 5 minutes.

Split Pea Soup

1 pound green split peas	½ raw carrot, diced
3 quarts water	½ cup raw, diced potato
1 medium onion, chopped	1 ham bone or ⅛ pound salt pork

1. Rinse peas. Place in kettle with rest of ingredients.
2. Bring to a boil and let simmer for about 3 hours. Season to taste. Add more water from time to time, if necessary.
3. Put through sieve, reheat and serve.

Minestrone

1 package minestrone soup mix	3 tablespoons dehydrated onion
3 quarts water	3 cups tomatoes, canned
1 ham bone	½ pound fresh spinach
1 clove garlic	

1. Soak minestrone soup mix overnight in water.
2. Add ham bone, garlic, onion, tomatoes. Cook several hours or until beans are tender. Correct seasoning.
3. When ready to serve, add spinach and cook 10 minutes.

Suggestion: Serve with fresh grated Parmesan cheese. This soup freezes well. Add spinach when ready to serve to preserve bright color.

Soup Italiano

1 can condensed pea soup
1 can condensed tomato soup
1½ cans water

2 tablespoons dry red wine
⅛ teaspoon Italian herb blend

1. Blend soups; add remaining ingredients.
2. Cook over low heat for 10 minutes. Serve with Italian Rye Chips. (see page 62)

Almond Soup

Serves 6

2 tablespoons melted butter
2 tablespoons cornstarch
5¼ cups chicken broth
1 cup heavy cream

1 cup finely chopped almonds
2 tablespoons finely chopped watercress leaves
Salt and pepper
½-1 teaspoon almond extract

1. Blend butter and cornstarch together until smooth. Stir in ½ cup chicken broth.
2. Heat remaining chicken broth and gradually stir into butter mixture.
3. Simmer soup for 5 minutes, stirring often.
4. Remove from heat and add cream and almonds. Allow to stand for 30 minutes for flavors to blend.
5. To serve, reheat soup. Add watercress, salt, pepper, and almond extract.

Can be made early in day and reheated.

Canadian Cheese Soup

Serves 4-6

¼ cup butter
1 small onion, minced
1 large carrot, diced
½ cup chopped celery
1 cup chicken broth
2 tablespoons flour

3 cups milk
¼ teaspoon Tabasco
Garlic salt
2 cups Black Diamond Cheddar, shredded
Chopped parsley

1. Sauté onion in butter until slightly soft. Add carrot, celery, and chicken broth; cover and simmer 15 minutes.
2. Put flour into 2 cup measure and add a little milk; mix thoroughly and fill to 2 cup mark, stirring until blended.
3. Add to soup; heat and stir until boiling and thickened.
4. Add cheese. Stir over low heat until melted. Season to taste with Tabasco and garlic salt.
5. Let set, off heat. When ready to serve, add remaining 1 cup milk and more chicken broth to taste. Reheat to just below boiling point before serving.
6. Sprinkle with chopped parsley. Serve with garlic toast points.

Egg Drop Soup

Serves 4

6 cups chicken soup
½ teaspoon sugar
½ teaspoon salt
Dash pepper

½ teaspoon MSG
1½ tablespoons cornstarch
¼ cup cold water
1 beaten egg

1. Combine first five ingredients in sauce pan; bring to boil and simmer 5 minutes.
2. Combine cornstarch and water, add to soup and stir well. Add beaten egg slowly.
3. Remove from heat. Stir and serve hot.

It's not a sin to use canned chicken soup!

Wonton Soup

6 uncooked filled wontons
1 can chicken broth or chicken stock
1 can water
1 tablespoon soy sauce
Dash of pepper

1 teaspoon sesame oil
Spinach, lettuce or other green vegetable, chopped
½ cup bamboo shoots, sliced
Salt to taste
1 tablespoon green onion, chopped

1. Boil wontons in water to cover. When done, they will float on top.
2. Combine chicken broth with remaining ingredients except onion and bring to a boil.
3. Place cooked wontons in individual bowls and pour chicken broth mixture over. Sprinkle with onion.

See Fried Wonton page 54. Prepare wrapper and proceed with filling instructions through step 5. At step 6 boil rather than fry. (See step 1 of Wonton Soup.)

Blender Black Bean Soup

6 servings (small bowls)

1 cup black beans
8 cups water
⅛ teaspoon mace
1 carrot, cut in pieces
1 onion, cut in pieces
1 small ham bone or ⅛ pound salt
   pork
¼ pound beef stew meat, cut in
   small pieces

Dash red pepper
2 cloves
2 hard cooked eggs, sliced thin
2 tablespoons sherry or lemon
   juice
½ lemon, sliced thin

1. Wash beans, cover with 2 cups water and soak overnight. In the morning drain water and discard.
2. Put carrot, onion and 2 cups water in blender container, cover and process at high speed on and off quickly several times to chop vegetables coarsely.
3. Pour into large saucepan. Add beans and remaining water, meat and seasoning. Cover and cook slowly about 3 hours or until beans are very soft.
4. Remove meat and cloves. Cool soup slightly.
5. Pour soup through a strainer, reserving stock.
6. Put vegetables into blender container, add stock to cover. Cover container and process at low speed to start, then turn control to high and process until smooth.
7. If mixture is too thick, add a little stock. Return puréed mixture, meat and reserved stock to soup kettle, add sherry or lemon juice and reheat.

Place in tureen; top with eggs and lemon slices.

This is very rich and thick. A little goes a long way.
For low cholesterol soup use egg whites only as garnish.

Cold Soups

Cold Purée Mongol

2 cans cream of tomato soup
2 cans beef consommé
2 cans split pea soup
2 soup cans milk
1 tablespoon grated onion

2 teaspoons allspice
Dash of curry powder
Chopped parsley
Sour cream
Seasoned croutons

1. Mix undiluted soups, milk, onion, allspice and curry powder with beater until well blended.
2. Chill in refrigerator several hours.
3. Serve in chilled mugs. Top with parsley, sour cream and croutons.

Quick Senegalese

Serves 4

1 can cream of chicken soup
1 can milk
½ teaspoon curry powder

1 cup chopped ice
Chives

1. Into the electric blender put the soup, milk and curry powder. Blend 10 to 15 seconds.
2. Add the ice and blend another 10 seconds or until blended.

Serve garnished with chopped chives in chilled mugs.

Smartini

1 can condensed cream of celery
  soup
1 soup can cracked ice

¼ cup chopped cucumbers, or to
  taste
¼ cup sour cream, or to taste
Dill weed

1. Combine all in blender and whirl smooth.
2. Sprinkle with dill for garnish.

This is a quickie summer soup that tastes similar to vichyssoise. It makes a nice cool drink as appetizer for a summer meal. Can be served in frosted glass with an olive.

Chlodnik

Low Calorie

Serves 6-8

½ bunch green onions
½ green pepper
1 cucumber, peeled and seeded
1 zucchini
¼ cup celery, chopped
¼ cup parsley, chopped
¼ cup watercress, chopped
½ cup dill pickle, chopped

¼ cup dill pickle juice
½ cup yogurt
1 quart buttermilk
1 teaspoon salt
1 teaspoon dill weed
Dash of garlic powder and black
   pepper
*2 cups shrimp or lump crabmeat

1. Mix all ingredients except seafood.
2. Run in batches in blender until smooth.
3. Chill thoroughly.
4. Just before serving, add shrimp or lump crabmeat.

Make a day ahead.

Serve from attractive tureen in chilled mugs in living room as first course.

Frosted Crab Soup

Serves 6

2 cans cream of vichyssoise soup   *1 6-ounce can crabmeat

1. Mix soup and drained crabmeat.
2. Chill until ready to serve.

Make ahead. Place in chilled cream soup dish or mug. This is similar to the famous frosted crab soup, served at The Suburban Club, Baltimore, Md.

4 cups vichyssoise (p. 151) can be substituted.

*See page 26.

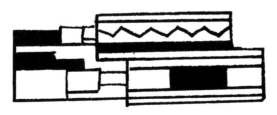

Chilled Avocado Soup

Serves 4 to 16

1 large, ripe avocado
2 cans clear consommé madrilene
1 cup sour cream

Salt, chili powder and cayenne to
  taste
Grated onion
Minced fresh dill or crushed dill
  seed

1. Peel avocado and remove seed. Whirl until smooth in electric blender or put through sieve or food mill.
2. Mix with consommé and sour cream.
3. Season with salt, chili powder, cayenne and onion.
4. Chill until mixture jells.

Serve in mugs or bouillon cups with garnish of dill.
Can be made a day ahead.

Watercress Soup

Serves 12

⅓ cup minced onion
3 tablespoons melted butter
3-4 cups watercress with stems,
  tightly packed

½ teaspoon salt
5½ cups chicken broth
3 tablespoons flour
½ cup whipping cream
2 egg yolks

1. Sauté onions in butter until tender but not brown. Stir in watercress and salt and cook slowly until tender, about 5 minutes.
2. Blend in blender with ½ cup chicken broth.
3. Stir flour into watercress mixture. Add remaining chicken broth and bring to boiling point, stirring occasionally to prevent lumps. Simmer 5 minutes.
4. Correct seasonings, and stir in whipping cream, into which egg yolks have been beaten.
5. Place saucepan over heat for a few minutes, simmer but don't boil. Cool and refrigerate.

Garnish with unsweetened whipped cream and watercress sprigs
and serve in chilled mugs. To serve hot, garnish with croutons.

Gazpacho I

1 46-ounce can tomato juice
½ cup chopped green onions
1 cup chopped green pepper
1-2 cups cubed, peeled tomatoes
⅛ teaspoon cayenne pepper

1-2 tablespoons salad oil
1 cup peeled, diced cucumber
1 cup diced celery
½ cup chopped parsley
⅛ teaspoon garlic salt

Mix all together and refrigerate.

Refreshing and delicious. Add croutons when serving (optional). Can be made day before serving. Good to keep in "frig" during summer.

Gazpacho II

Serves 8

1 clove garlic
2 tablespoons salad oil
2 medium onions, chopped
1 green pepper, chopped
1 cucumber, chopped
4 stalks celery, chopped
3 medium tomatoes, peeled and
   chopped

2 teaspoons salt
1 teaspoon freshly ground pepper
2 teaspoons Worcestershire
½ cup vinegar
3 cups tomato juice
1 handful fresh dill or parsley,
   chopped

1. Press garlic into large bowl. Stir in oil.
2. Chop vegetables with sharp knife (not by machine), and add them to the oil as they are being chopped.
3. Stir in seasonings, vinegar and tomato juice.
4. Cover tightly and refrigerate for use the next day.
5. Add fresh dill just before serving.

Prepare, store and serve in same pot (but be sure the lid is tight). Everyone always wants to know the exotic origin of this really refreshing, crunchy soup. It was adapted from The Cincinnati Enquirer.

Cold Bold Tomato Soup

Serves 6

3 cups seasoned tomato juice
¾ cup sour cream
½ cucumber

¼ cup celery
Green onion to garnish
Whole ground pepper

1. Blend tomato juice and sour cream.
2. Slice cucumber and celery as thin as possible. Add to tomato juice.
3. Chill soup.
4. Garnish with onions and pepper when serving.

Suggestion: Serve in chilled mugs away from table.

Fresh Chilled Tomato Soup

Serves 4

6 medium sized tomatoes
¼ cup fresh lemon juice
¼ cup salad oil
Salt to taste

Ground black pepper
Onion powder
3 drops Tabasco
1 cup sour cream
½ teaspoon curry powder

1. Dip the tomatoes in boiling water for about thirty seconds; remove skins.
2. Cut up tomatoes and put in a blender at medium speed for a few seconds, until you have a coarse purée and the seeds are ground up.
3. Mix in the lemon juice and oil. Add salt (start with ½ teaspoon), ground black pepper, onion powder all to taste and put in the hot pepper sauce. Mix all together with a spoon.
4. Place in the refrigerator to chill for at least eight hours.
5. When ready to serve, mix curry powder, salt and pepper to taste with the sour cream. Place the soup in bowls and garnish by floating a tablespoon of the seasoned sour cream in each bowl.

This is a delightful summer soup and is similar to gazpacho yet it is more delicate and unusual. The seasoning of this soup can vary depending on the tastes of the chef.

Vichyssoise

¼ cup butter or margarine
2 onions, finely chopped
1½ cups chopped leeks or
   scallions, including green tops
3½ cups chicken broth

3 potatoes, quartered
*2 cups light cream
1 teaspoon salt
½ teaspoon white pepper
2 tablespoons chopped chives

1. Sauté onions and scallions in butter slowly until onions are transparent but not brown. Add 1¾ cups chicken broth, simmer 10 to 15 minutes and allow to cool.
2. Cook the potatoes in 1¾ cups chicken broth until soft. Cool.
3. Put vegetables and broth through food mill or smooth in blender to obtain a very smooth mixture.
4. Add cream, salt, pepper. Mix well.
5. Refrigerate overnight.
6. Serve cold topped with chives.

Thin to desired consistency with additional cream or buttermilk.

*For a zesty flavor substitute 1 cup of sour cream for 1 cup light cream.

Easy Vichyssoise

Serves 3

1 can vichyssoise
Salt and pepper to taste

½ cup chive sour cream

1. Mix thoroughly.
2. Chill.

Serve with an additional teaspoon of chive sour cream on top of each serving.

Instant Vichyssoise

Serves 8 to 10

1. Use two packages of Knorr Potato Leek Soup. Follow recipe on package for vichyssoise, substituting 2% milk.
2. When cool, put in blender with diet or imitation sour cream.

Serve cold from punch bowl in chilled cups. Garnish with diced spring onions.

Cold Beet Borscht

Serves 4

1 can bouillon or consommé
½ dill pickle
⅓ cucumber
1 8-ounce can julienne beets

1 tablespoon lemon juice
2 tablespoons pickle juice
Sugar to taste
4 ice cubes

1. In blender pour bouillon, the juice and half the solid contents of julienne beets (reserve the rest for adding later), dill pickle, cucumber, lemon juice, sugar or sweetener if desired, pickle juice, and ice cubes. Blend smooth.
2. Add rest of slivered beets and chill.

Serve with sour cream or Mock Sour Cream (page 131) in chilled mugs.

Beet And Buttermilk Soup

Serves 8

2 8½-ounce cans whole tiny beets
1 quart fresh buttermilk

Salt and pepper to taste
3 tablespoons finely cut fresh chives

1. Purée beets.
2. Combine beets and buttermilk.
3. Season to taste with freshly ground pepper and salt.
4. Let stand in refrigerator 2-3 hours.
5. Pour into mugs and sprinkle top with finely cut chives.

No calories — well, hardly any — and can be made a day ahead.

Fruit Soup

Serves 8

1 pound raspberries, plums or sour cherries
2 eggs, separated

2 tablespoons cornstarch
⅛ teaspoon salt
2 tablespoons sugar
Lemon rind

1. Heat fruit and an equal amount of water to boiling point; strain and reserve fruit.
2. Combine egg yolks, cornstarch and enough water to make a thin mixture.
3. Add to soup, stirring constantly, Bring to boil and cook 3 minutes. Combine soup and reserved fruit.
4. Add sugar to taste. Cool.
5. Just before serving, beat egg whites with sugar, salt and a little grated lemon rind. Drop by spoonfuls to float on top of soup.

A refreshing unusual first course for a luncheon. Serve in chilled mugs.

Jellied Soups

Jellied Gazpacho
Low Calorie

Serves 4

1 can gazpacho
1 tablespoon unflavored gelatin

1 can jellied consommé

1. Soften gelatin in ½ cup cold gazpacho.
2. Add gelatin mixture to rest of boiling gazpacho soup.
3. When thoroughly dissolved, add consommé to the gazpacho. Mix together.
4. Place in a bowl in the refrigerator until set.

Only 29 calories per serving!

2 cups of Gazpacho (p. 149) can be jelled by adding one package (1 tablespoon) softened and dissolved unflavored gelatin.

Jellied Madrilene in Avocado Shell

Avocados
French dressing
Madrilene

Sour cream
Caviar
Lemon wedges

1. Cut ripe avocado in half; remove seed.
2. Spread 1 teaspoon French dressing over avocado.
3. Spoon jellied madrilene into shell.
4. Chill until madrilene is well set.

When ready to serve, top with 1 tablespoon sour cream and a little caviar. Serve with lemon wedge. May be sliced in quarters when well chilled.

Jellied Tomato Olive Soup
Low Calorie

Serves 4

2 cans madrilene
¼ cup chopped green olives

1 cup diced tomato, well drained
Mock sour cream

1. Chill madrilene until practically jelled.
2. Fold in well drained tomato and olives.
3. Pour into soup cups.
4. Top with 1 tablespoon Mock Sour Cream* (page 131) and sprinkle with capers or caviar.

This is a mild, delicately flavored soup. For a more highly seasoned soup you may also add:

½ cup finely chopped green pepper
2 tablespoons finely chopped onion
⅛ teaspoon red hot sauce

Jellied Clam Tomato Soup
(Low Calorie)

Serves 4

2 cans madrilene
1 can minced clams, well-drained

Mock sour cream
Capers or caviar

1. Chill madrilene until practically jelled.
2. Fold in well-drained clams. Pour into mugs.
3. Top with 1 tablespoon Mock Sour Cream* (page 131) and sprinkle with capers or caviar.

*If you can afford the calories use real sour cream!

Ready and Bready

A wonderful pick from the flour garden. Sift through the party loaves and pretzels to a harvest of hurrahs.

12

Pretzels

1 envelope dry yeast
1½ cups warm water
4 to 5 cups flour
Pinch of salt

Pinch of sugar
1 quart water
2 tablespoons baking soda
Coarse salt

1. Dissolve yeast in ¼ cup warm water. Add remaining water.
2. Stir in 4 cups flour, salt and sugar. If necessary, add more flour for stiff (not sticky) dough.
3. Knead until smooth and elastic.
4. Form dough into a ball. Place in greased bowl. Spread lightly with soft butter.
5. Cover with towel and let rise in warm place for about 45 minutes. (It rises about one-half itself.)
6. Pinch off small ball of dough. Roll between hands to form a 20-inch long, ¼ to ½ inch wide strip. Form into pretzel shape, wetting ends and pinching together.
7. Bring 1 quart water and 2 tablespoons baking soda to a boil. Dip pretzels, let boil 1 minute or until pretzel floats.
8. Remove with pancake turner and drain.
9. Place drained pretzel on buttered, foiled baking sheets. Sprinkle heavily with coarse salt.
10. Bake in 400° oven 15 minutes or until golden brown. Cool on wire rack.

Pretzels can be frozen after boiling and draining. Apply salt and bake when needed. Great with drinks. Serve with mustard.

Beer Biscuits

2 cups biscuit mix
½ cup cheddar, grated

½ cup beer

1. Blend all ingredients.
2. Knead 5 times on floured board.
3. Roll into a rectangle, 4 inches wide and ½ inch thick.
4. Cut into about 8 triangles.
5. Bake 8 to 10 minutes at 450°. Cool on wire rack.

Cracker Puffs

Saltines   Butter
Sesame seeds, caraway, or dill seed

1. Soak saltines in cold water for 20 minutes.
2. Lift from water with perforated pancake turner, allowing water to drain off.
3. Place on greased cookie sheet 1½ inches apart.
4. Sprinkle with sesame seed, caraway or dill seed.
5. Put a ½ teaspoon pat of butter on top of each cracker.
6. Bake at 400° for half an hour without opening oven door. They will be brown, crisp and puffed.
7. Cool on wire rack.
8. Store in airtight can.
9. Reheat to crisp before using.

Party Mix

6 tablespoons butter
4 teaspoons Worcestershire
1 teaspoon seasoned salt
4 cups assorted—
    Wheat Chex, Corn Chex, Rice
    Chex or pretzel sticks

2 cups assorted—
    sunflower seeds (shelled), toasted
    soy beans, pumpkin seeds
    (hulled)
¾ cup salted nuts

1. Melt butter in heavy skillet, over low heat. Stir in Worcestershire and salt.
2. Add assorted seeds, cereals and nuts. Mix over low heat until all are coated.
3. Spread out on large cookie sheet.
4. Bake 45 minutes in 250° oven.
5. Place on paper towels to cool.
6. Store in airtight can.

Garlic Cheese Breadsticks

2 packages breadsticks
¼ pound butter (more if
    necessary)

1 tablespoon garlic powder
1 tablespoon Parmesan cheese

1. Melt butter in skillet.
2. Mix in cheese and garlic powder.
3. Roll breadsticks in butter mixture or brush with pastry brush.
4. Bake at 400° for 5 to 10 minutes.
5. Remove to wire rack to cool.
6. Store in airtight can.

Any other seasonings may be substituted for garlic and cheese.

Roquefort Cheese Bread

1 loaf French bread
¼ pound sweet butter

6 ounces Roquefort cheese

1. Slice French bread thinly.
2. Mix butter and Roquefort cheese together in bowl.
3. Thickly spread mixture on slices of bread, putting them back together in loaf form.
4. Wrap in aluminum foil and freeze.
5. Bake at 350° to serve very hot. (Bake in the same aluminum foil.)

French Bread Fantasy

French bread
1 cup mayonnaise
1 teaspoon Worcestershire
½ clove garlic, chopped

Salt and pepper to taste
1 3-ounce package cream cheese
3 or 4 scallions, chopped

1. Slice French bread 1 inch thick.
2. Mix mayonnaise with garlic and other seasonings.
3. Beat mayonnaise mixture into softened cream cheese and chopped scallions (including the green part).
4. Spread on French bread.
5. Broil a few minutes.

Note: This can be made ahead and refrigerated. Broil when ready to serve.

Onion Dipped Bread

1 loaf Italian or French bread
½ cup butter or margarine, softened

1 envelope toasted onion dip mix
Parmesan cheese

1. Cut loaf in half lengthwise.
2. Blend butter and onion dip mix.
3. Spread on bread. Sprinkle with Parmesan cheese. Cut into finger strips.
4. Bake at 425° for 10 minutes.

Delicious and so easy!

Melba Toast

White bread   Seasoned salt (optional)
Butter

1. Freeze a loaf of white bread.
2. Cut crust off one end.
3. Spread lightly with softened butter.
4. Cut off thin slice.
5. Continue buttering end and cutting off slices until loaf is used.
6. Lay slices on cookie sheet.
7. Bake at 250° until dried out and lightly browned.

For a zesty flavor, sprinkle with seasoned salt.

Rye Melba Toast

Party rye   Butter
                             Seasoned salt

1. Butter thin party rye. Sprinkle with seasoned salt.
2. Bake at 200° for 2 hours or until dried and crisp.

Sandwich Loaves

Riviera Loaf

Serves 8

1 loaf French bread
1 pound ground beef
⅓ cup grated Parmesan cheese
¼ cup chopped onion
¼ cup chopped olives
1 teaspoon salt

½ teaspoon oregano
Dash pepper
1 6-ounce can tomato paste
2 tomatoes, thinly sliced
5 slices sharp Old English cheese,
   cut in triangles

1. Cut loaf in half lengthwise.
2. Combine meat with Parmesan cheese, onion, olives, seasonings and tomato paste.
3. Spread evenly and to the edges of each half loaf.
4. Broil about 5 inches from heat for 10 minutes (less for rare).
5. Top with tomato and cheese slices. Broil 1-2 minutes, just until cheese begins to melt.
6. Slice and serve.

Suggestions: Good on English muffin halves, leaving the cheese in whole slices. Excellent for midnight snack with coffee.

Sandwich Loaf or Ribbon Sandwich

Serves 10 to 12

1 pound unsliced white bread
*3 fillings (egg salad, marinated
   tomatoes, tuna fish)
Butter for spreading

1 8-ounce package cream cheese
Milk to thin cheese
Parsley, carrots and pimiento for
   decoration

1. Cut crusts from loaf of bread. Cut loaf into 4 lengthwise slices.
2. Butter each inside slice to keep it from splitting apart later when cut vertically to be served.
3. Make 3 fillings.
4. Spread one filling on each layer. Stack into loaf.
5. Wrap with moist towel and chill.
6. Soften cream cheese in mixing bowl. Beat cream cheese until smooth, add milk until desired spreading consistency.
7. About 3 hours before serving, spread on top and sides of loaf.
8. Decorate with flowers made from parsley, pimiento and carrots.

Suggestions: Can be made the day before and frosted just prior to serving.

*For other fillings, prepare any of deviled egg fillings (pages 87-90). Adjust mayonnaise to spreading consistency.

Sip and Sup

Another kind of toast. A marvelous group of party drinks that are perfect companions to hors d'oeuvres. A sure way to add punch and sizzle to a gathering.

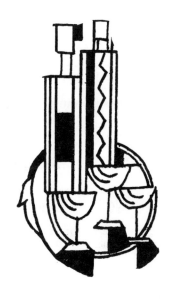

13

The Laughing Fish® Cocktail

1 ounce 151 rum
½ ounce applejack brandy
½ ounce apricot brandy
¼ ounce Rose's lime

Orange juice
Orange slice
Cherry

1. Pour rum and applejack brandy into highball glass.
2. Add ice to glass, fill one inch from top with orange juice.
3. Add Rose's lime. Top with apricot brandy. Stir.
4. Garnish with orange slice and cherry.

As created by and served at Holiday Inn of Pompano Beach, Florida, Holiday Inn of Fort Lauderdale-West, Florida, and Sheraton of Boca Raton, Florida.

Sangria Cherrington

2 litres Chardonnay
32 ounces club soda
Green grapes
Kiwi fruit

3 limes, sliced
1 box fresh strawberries
3 lemons, sliced
3 oranges, sliced
Sugar if desired

Combine above ingredients in two glass pitchers and enjoy.

—Cherrington's Restaurant, Cincinnati

Sangria

Serves 10

1 fifth of medium dry Spanish Red
   Burgundy
3 juice oranges, squeezed for juice
1 ounce Grand Marnier
1 apple, sliced

1 lemon, sliced
1 orange halved and sliced
6 ounces club soda

1. Mix wine and orange juice in ½ gallon pitcher.
2. Add Grand Marnier and fruit slices.
3. When ready to serve, add club soda and ice cubes.

Fortune Kookie

1½ ounces brandy
1½ ounces vodka
1 ounce Rose's lime juice

1 dash bitters
7 Up

1. Pour first four ingredients in tall glass.
2. Fill glass with ice cubes and 7 Up.

—The Fortune Kookie Restaurant, Cincinnati.

Peach with a Punch

Makes 4 cups

1 10-ounce package frozen peach
slices, partially thawed
1 6-ounce can frozen lemonade
concentrate, partially thawed

⅔ cup vodka
12 ice cubes

1. In blender container, combine peaches, lemonade and vodka.
Cover and blend till chopped.
2. Add ice cubes, one at a time, blending until slushy. Pour into
a punch bowl; garnish with maraschino cherries and lemon
wedges, if desired.

Back Bay Bombers

Serves 12

12 ounces apricot brandy
9 cups cranberry juice, chilled
9 cups orange juice, chilled

1. Mix ingredients together.
2. Pour in glasses or punch bowl and garnish with orange slices

St. Gregory Sunrise

1 shot vodka
Cranberry juice

Orange juice
Lime juice

Pour vodka and equal amounts of juices over ice in tall glass.
Finish with a squeeze of lime.

—St. Gregory's Restaurant, Cincinnati

Bourbon Slush

Serves 10-12

2 tea bags
2 cups boiling water
½ cup sugar (optional)
2 6-ounce cans frozen orange juice
    concentrate

2 6-ounce cans frozen lemonade
    concentrate
3 cups water
2 cups bourbon
Cherries, strawberries or orange
    slices

1. Add tea bags to boiling water and brew 3 to 5 minutes. Allow to cool.
2. Add sugar, if wanted.
3. Mix remaining ingredients with the brewed tea.
4. Put into container and store in freezer until it becomes slushy.

Serve in low fancy cocktail glasses (you can drink it as it starts to melt). Garnish with red cherry, strawberry, or orange slice.

Easy Whiskey Sours

Serves 4-6

1 6-ounce can frozen lemonade
12 ounces Canada Dry Wink

6 ounces bourbon
Cherries and orange slices for
    garnish

Mix Wink, lemonade and bourbon. Chill.

Serve over ice with garnish. May be made 3-4 hours before serving.

Southern Comfort Punch

Serves 25

2½ cups Southern Comfort
2¼ quarts 7-Up
6 ounces lemon juice

1 6-ounce can frozen orange juice
    (unsweetened)
2 6-ounce cans frozen lemonade

Combine all ingredients in punch bowl.

Serve with decorated ice ring made of ice, orange juice, lemonade or combination of all.

Sicilian Kiss

1 ounce Amaretto

1 ounce Southern Comfort

Mix.

—Ciuccio's Restaurant, Cincinnati

Banana Daiquiri I

2-3 servings

1 banana, cut up
3 tablespons fresh lemon juice
6 tablespoons light rum

2 tablespoons sugar, or to taste
Crushed ice
Mint leaves
Banana slices

1. Place first four ingredients in blender; blend at high speed for 30 seconds.
2. Gradually blend in crushed ice until slushy. Pour into stemmed glasses; garnish with mint leaves and banana slices.

Banana Daiquiri II

Serves 2

2 ounces rum
2 teaspoons lime juice or
   2 teaspoons lemon juice

1 ounce crème de banana
1 banana, peeled

Place all ingredients in blender; whip until creamy.

Long Island Ice Tea

¾ ounce bourbon
¾ ounce rum
¾ ounce vodka
2 ounces bar lemon

¼ ounce triple sec
3 ounces Pepsi
Lemon wedge

1. Blend together first 5 ingredients.
2. Pour over ice in tall glass and top with Pepsi and lemon wedge.

—The Pavilion Restaurant, Cincinnati

Snow on the Mountain

1½ ounces Vandermint
1½ ounces white crème de cacao

1½ ounces cream

Shake and strain. Serve in short glass.

—Adrica's Restaurant, Cincinnati

Southern Eggnog

12 eggs, separated
1¼ cup sugar
¼ teaspoon salt
3 cups half and half

1 cup or more bourbon (to taste)
½ cup light rum
1 quart whipping cream
Freshly grated nutmeg

1. Chill the whipping cream in the freezer until partially frozen—about 20 minutes.
2. Beat egg whites and salt until stiff. Beat in ¾ cup sugar, one tablespoon at a time. Continue beating to form a meringue-like consistency.
3. Beat egg yolks and remaining sugar, until thick and lemon colored. Add bourbon, rum and half and half to egg yolk mixture.
4. Fold beaten egg whites into egg yolk mixture.
5. Whip cream until stiff. Fold into egg mixture. Add more bourbon if desired.

Serve in chilled punch bowl. Top each serving with a little freshly-grated nutmeg.

Extra Special, Extra Easy Egg Nog

Serves 8-12

1 quart vanilla ice cream*
1½ cups brandy

Freshly grated nutmeg

1. Soften vanilla ice cream.
2. Mix in brandy.

Serve in fancy punch cups. Sprinkle freshly grated nutmeg on top.

*The best you can afford.

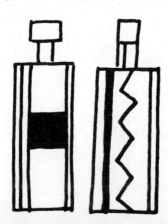

Benihana Punch

8 ounces passion fruit juice
8 ounces kalupico (Japanese juice)
8 ounces grenadine
10 ounces sour mix

½ ounce peach liquer
½ ounce rum
48 ounces orange juice
48 ounces pineapple juice

Mix in punch bowl.

—Benihana Restaurant, Cincinnati.

Piña Colada

For each serving:
  1 ounce cream of coconut
  2 ounces unsweetened pineapple juice
  1½ ounces rum
  ½ cup crushed ice

Put all ingredients in blender and blend until frothy.

Freeze unused cream of coconut.

Heritage Hunkar Hurricane

1 ounce Grand Mariner
½ ounce Triple Sec

1½ ounces Cocoanut Cream (Coco Lopez)
1 scoop vanilla ice cream

1. Blend all ingredients and pour into a tall wine glass.
2. Garnish with piece of pineapple.

This recipe is from a Heritage patron named Denes Hunkar who came to Cincinnati from Hungary.

—The Heritage, Cincinnati.

Edward's Bloody Mary

1 quart V-8 or tomato juice
2½ teaspoons horseradish
4½ teaspoons Worcestershire
½ teaspoon cayenne pepper
¾ teaspoon salt
6 ounces vodka

½ teaspoon seasoned pepper
½ teaspoon lemon pepper
¾ ounce lemon juice
¼ ounce Rose's lime juice
Celery or cucumber
Lime wedges

Mix first 9 ingredients. Serve over ice with celery or cucumber garnish and lime wedge.

This makes one pitcher.

—Edward's Restaurant, Cincinnati

Bloody Mary

Serves 10-12 (½ gallon)

46 ounces tomato juice
1 10½-ounce can bouillon
3 ounces lime juice
¼ cup Worcestershire
½-2 teaspoons hot pepper sauce
1 quart vodka

2 teaspoons coarse salt
1 teaspoon coarse pepper
1 teaspoon celery salt
1 teaspoon dill weed
2 teaspoons horseradish (prepared)

1. Combine ingredients and mix well. Put in gallon jug.
2. Chill overnight.
3. Fill 12 ounce glasses with ice cubes. Add mixture. Garnish with cucumber slice, lime wedge or celery stalk.

Hot Drinks

Swedish Glögg

⅓-½ cup sugar (depends on
    sweetness of wine)
1 3-inch strip orange peel
1 3-inch strip lemon peel
3 sticks cinnamon
1 teaspoon whole cloves
⅓ cup blanched almonds

¼ cup raisins
¼ teaspoon angostura bitters
4 pods cardamon seed
1 pint light port wine
1 pint sherry
1 cup blackberry brandy

Combine all ingredients and heat over low heat until very hot,
but do not boil. Hold at this temperature for 10 minutes.

Serve hot. Spoon some almonds and raisins with each serving.

Great on a cold night by the fire!

Glögg (Glug)

⅓-½ cup sugar
3-4 inch strips of lemon peel
1 teaspoon whole cloves
1 teaspoon bitters
4 pods cardimon seeds
1 pint clear Burgundy

1 pint sherry
1 cup brandy
¼ cup raisins
Peeled almonds
3 inch cinnamon sticks for stirring

1. Mix all ingredients together except almonds and cinnamon.
2. Heat, covered, until simmering.
3. Strain.
4. Drop peeled almonds into cups. Pour in Glögg and serve with
   cinnamon sticks. Serve hot.

Hot Fruit Punch

4 servings

1 cup water
¼ cup sugar
8 whole allspice
8 cloves
2 3-inch pieces cinnamon stick
1½ cups unsweetened pineapple
    juice

1 cup grapefruit juice
1 cup orange juice
¼ cup lemon juice
6 ounces gin
Orange slices

1. Combine water, sugar, and spices in a saucepan. Simmer for 10
   minutes.
2. Add fruit juices and gin; heat but do not boil.
3. Strain the punch into mugs and garnish each with an orange
   slice.

169

Mulled Wine

10-12 servings

4 cups water
½ cup sugar
12 cloves

1 3-inch piece cinnamon stick
Peel of 2 oranges
Peel of one lemon
2 bottles dry red wine

1. In a large saucepan, mix the first six ingredients; boil for fifteen minutes.
2. Strain mixture and return to saucepan; add the wine. Heat, but do not let it boil.
3. Serve in warmed mugs.

Wassail

20 servings

1 32-ounce bottle cranberry juice
    cocktail
2 cups apple juice
1 cup sugar
6 inches of stick cinnamon, broken

24 whole cloves
12 whole allspice
1 lemon, sliced
6½ cups (two fifths) dry red wine

1. In 4-quart bowl, combine juices and sugar.
2. Tie spices in cheesecloth bag; add to bowl along with sliced lemon.
3. Place in microwave; cook at HIGH for 10 minutes or until almost boiling.
4. Add wine. Cook at HIGH for 15 minutes or until heated through.
5. Remove spice bag. Serve hot in mugs.

Hot Spiced Wine

Makes 12 drinks

2 3-inch pieces stick cinnamon
1 nutmeg, crushed
8 cloves

8 cups red wine
Peel of 2 lemons
Peel of 2 oranges

1. In a piece of cheesecloth, place cinnamon, nutmeg and cloves. Tie into a bag.
2. Place spice bag, wine, lemon and orange peel in a large saucepan. Heat the wine, but do not let it boil.
3. Discard the spice bag and fruit peels; serve in warmed mugs.

Café au Grand Marnier

For each serving:

1½ ounces Grand Marnier
¾ cup freshly perked coffee
Whipped cream

1. Fill mug ¾ full with coffee.
2. Pour Grand Marnier into cup.
3. Top with whipped cream.

A delightful alternative to IRISH COFFEE!

Prizewinning R.S.V.P. Irish Coffee

Use freshly ground black coffee.

Use only fresh half and half. Shake it until your arms ache; do not cheat by using a blender or beater.

Sweeten coffee with light brown sugar.

Use NO cinnamon.

One shot of John Jameson Irish Whiskey. No other.

Chill the spoon used to float cream over the top. If you do it exactly right, the cream will stripe.

This recipe from RSVP Restaurant won at the annual St. Patrick's Day Irish Coffee contest in Cincinnati.

—RSVP Restaurant, Cincinnati.

Bavarian Mint

1 shot of peppermint schnapps   1 shot light creme de cacao

1. Add above ingredients to cup of hot chocolate, served in tulip glass.
2. Garnish with whipped cream, cinnamon, cherry.

A specialty of Rusconi's Restaurant.

Hot Buttered Rum

Makes 10-12 drinks

½ cup butter
½ cup dark brown sugar
½ teaspoon nutmeg
½ teaspoon cinnamon

¼ teaspoon ground cloves
Pinch of salt
2½ to 3 cups dark rum
Hot water

1. In a bowl, beat butter and sugar until light and fluffy. Add spices and blend well.
2. Place 2 teaspoons of the butter mixture in each warm mug.
3. Add ¼ cup rum to each mug and fill with hot water. Serve warm.

Non Alcoholic

Orange Renée

Serves 6 to 8

1 cup orange juice
1 cup milk*
½ cup sugar

2 teaspoons vanilla
1 cup ice water
10 ice cubes

1. Place ingredients except ice in blender; process or blend at high speed for 15 seconds.
2. Add ice cubes, one at a time. Blend at low speed until slushy.

For richer drink you can use half and half

Bride's Pink Punch

Serves 35

1 3-ounce package strawberry
   gelatin
1 cup boiling water
1 package strawberry Kool-Aid,
   unsweetened

1½ cups sugar
2 quarts water
1 46-ounce can pineapple juice
1 10-ounce bottle 7-Up
2 pints pineapple sherbet

1. Dissolve gelatin in boiling water.
2. Dissolve Kool-Aid mix in cold water. Add sugar and stir well.
3. Add pineapple juice and gelatin. (May be made ahead to this point and stored in a one gallon container.)
4. Add 7-Up and sherbet just before serving.

May be spiked if desired.

Fruit Punch

Serves 50

5 pounds sugar (10 cups)
½ gallon strong tea
1 46-ounce can unsweeteneed
   grapefruit juice
1 46-ounce can unsweetened
   pineapple juice

1 40-ounce bottle unsweetened
   grape juice
6 oranges, sliced
6 lemons, sliced

1. Dissolve sugar in hot tea. Add other ingredients.
2. Pour over ice ring in punch bowl.*
3. Garnish with orange and lemon slices.

See Holiday Punch, page 173 for method to make Ice Ring.

Holiday Punch

36 ½-cup servings

6 cups cranberry juice, chilled
3 cups apple juice, chilled
¾ cup lemon juice, chilled

1½ cups orange juice, chilled
2 28-ounce bottles ginger ale, chilled

1. Combine fruit juices in punch bowl.
2. Just before serving, pour in ginger ale; stir well.
3. Garnish with ice ring.

To make ice ring:
1. Fill a ring mold half full of cold water and freeze until solid.
2. Arrange one or more of the following fruits in a design over the surface of the ice: maraschino cherries, mandarin orange slices, pineapple chunks, lemon or lime slices.
3. Cover fruits with water and freeze.
4. To unmold, dip in warm water.

Snowman Punch

Serves 20

2 cups water
½ cup sugar
12 whole cloves
2 sticks cinnamon

3 pints cranberry juice
1 6-ounce can lemonade
1 6-ounce can orange juice

1. Bring water, sugar, cloves and cinnamon to boil. Stir to dissolve sugar.
2. Simmer 5 minutes; cool. Remove spices.
3. Mix syrup mixture with juices. Serve over ice.

Citrus Refresher

Makes 4½ quarts

2 6-ounce cans lemonade (frozen)
1 6-ounce can orange juice (frozen)
2 cups pineapple juice

3½ quarts ice water
5 tablespoons instant tea

Mix.

Creamy Coffee Punch

Serves 30

4 quarts cold strong coffee
1 quart cold milk
1 tablespoon vanilla

1 cup sugar
2 quarts vanilla ice cream
Whipped cream

1. Combine coffee, milk and vanilla.
2. Add sugar and stir until dissolved. Chill thoroughly.
3. Pour over ice cream in punch bowl.
4. Serve in punch cups, topped with a dollop of whipped cream, if desired.

Steps 1 and 2 may be done the day before.

Great for a morning coffee.

This recipe was contributed by Tommye Miller, food editor of the Mobile (AL) Press.

Cranberry Punch

Place in percolator basket of coffee pot
2 tablespoons whole cloves
1 tablespoon whole allspice
5 sticks cinnamon
½ cup brown sugar

Place in bottom of coffee pot
1 large can cranberry juice
1 large can pineapple juice
1 large can water

Perk as though making coffee. Use 20 cup coffee pot or larger.

Good hot drink.

Index Table of Contents

Index

ETHNIC

182

186

HORS D'OEUVRES, HOT

194

SOUR CREAM & YOGURT

VEGETABLES
Artichokes
Asparagus
Avocado
Beans
Beets
Brussel Sprouts
Cabbage
Carrots
Cauliflower
Celery

If you are enjoying your copy of IN THE BEGINNING, you will love BEGINNING AGAIN, our newest hors d'oeuvre cookbook. With both books in your kitchen, you will own the most comprehensive party planning ideas ever published.

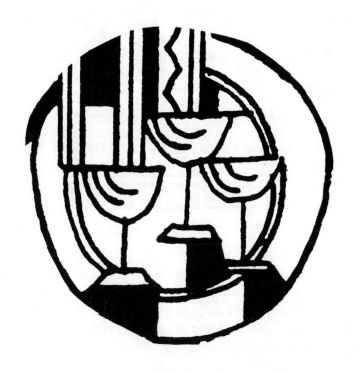

ORDER FORM

I would like to order _____ copies of IN THE BEGINNING
I would like to order _____ copies of BEGINNING AGAIN
Price $8.95 plus $1.75 handling
    Ohio State Residents add 50¢ sales tax
    Outside continental United States add $1.00 per book

Enclosed is my check for $_____

PLEASE PRINT OR TYPE

Name_____

Address_____

City, State_____ Zip_____

Gift card message_____

....

I would like to order _____ copies of IN THE BEGINNING
I would like to order _____ copies of BEGINNING AGAIN
Price $8.95 plus $1.75 handling
    Ohio State Residents add 50¢ sales tax
    Outside continental United States add $1.00 per book

Enclosed is my check for $_____

PLEASE PRINT OR TYPE

Name_____

Address_____

City, State_____ Zip_____

Gift card message_____

....

I would like to order _____ copies of IN THE BEGINNING
I would like to order _____ copies of BEGINNING AGAIN
Price $8.95 plus $1.75 handling
    Ohio State Residents add 50¢ sales tax
    Outside continental United States add $1.00 per book

Enclosed is my check for $_____

PLEASE PRINT OR TYPE

Name_____

Address_____

City, State_____ Zip_____

Gift card message_____

....

Please mail all orders and checks to: ROCKDALE RIDGE PRESS
                Dept. ITB
                P.O. Box 37848
                Cincinnati, Ohio 45222
                (513)891-9900

ORDER FORM

I would like to order _____ copies of IN THE BEGINNING
I would like to order _____ copies of BEGINNING AGAIN
Price $8.95 plus $1.75 handling
      Ohio State Residents add 50¢ sales tax
      Outside continental United States add $1.00 per book

Enclosed is my check for $_____

PLEASE PRINT OR TYPE

Name_____

Address_____

City, State_____ Zip_____

Gift card message_____

_____

....

I would like to order _____ copies of IN THE BEGINNING
I would like to order _____ copies of BEGINNING AGAIN
Price $8.95 plus $1.75 handling
      Ohio State Residents add 50¢ sales tax
      Outside continental United States add $1.00 per book

Enclosed is my check for $_____

PLEASE PRINT OR TYPE

Name_____

Address_____

City, State_____ Zip_____

Gift card message_____

_____

....

I would like to order _____ copies of IN THE BEGINNING
I would like to order _____ copies of BEGINNING AGAIN
Price $8.95 plus $1.75 handling
      Ohio State Residents add 50¢ sales tax
      Outside continental United States add $1.00 per book

Enclosed is my check for $_____

PLEASE PRINT OR TYPE

Name_____

Address_____

City, State_____ Zip_____

Gift card message_____

_____

....

Please mail all orders and checks to: ROCKDALE RIDGE PRESS
                                        Dept. ITB
                                        P.O. Box 37848
                                        Cincinnati, Ohio 45222
                                        (513)891-9900